Contents

MULTI-MEDIA IN THE CHURCH

A BEGINNER'S GUIDE FOR PUTTING IT ALL TOGETHER

W. A. ENGSTROM

JOHN KNOX PRESS
Richmond, Virginia

Library of Congress Cataloging in Publication Data

Engstrom, W   A   1925-
    Multi-media in the church.

    Bibliography: p.
    1. Church work--Audio-visual aids. 2. Public
worship. I. Title.
BV1535.E55   254'.6   72-11165
ISBN 0-8042-1730-0

Acknowledgments

To my family, who consented to my leaving the security of the pastorate to enroll in the graduate school of the University of Texas.

To Dr. DeWitt Reddick for his encouragement to pursue graduate studies; to Dr. Stanley Donner and Dr. Rod Whitaker for encouraging me to pursue the writing of the book, and a special note of thanks to Dr. Robert Brooks, who worked patiently with me in the writing of the manuscript.

An expression of deep gratitude is due Harry Garner, who did the illustrations while a student in the University of Texas School of Architecture.

I will always be indebted to the members of the Hyde Park Presbyterian Church for their understanding and patience and for their encouragement in developing this concept of worship.

Illustrations

Introduction

We live in a vivid world. New emphasis on color and sound seems to be everywhere. The sights and sounds of film and television transport us into unknown worlds.

Most of our worship takes place in sanctuaries designed to remove us from the world as much as possible through architecture, the clothes worn by the minister and the people, the language used, the music that is sung, and the lack of dialogue and conversation which are at the center of meaningful relationships between people.

It is possible to change the environment of worship by means of sight and sound adjustments. Church architecture can also be modified and adapted by the creative use of sight and sound.

It is possible to bring the sights and sounds of the world into our sanctuaries so that we might once again experience the blending of work and worship, of play and prayer.

One means of renewal of worship is the use of multi-media forms. Multi-media is the blending of two or more media forms into an integrated whole.

A minister is a form of multi-media. As he blends sight (how he looks, both standing and moving) and sound (the sounds he makes in speaking) into a unity, he is either in good media form or, in some cases, in bad form. Some part of his presence may detract from his total appearance.

A minister is able to use media as an extension of himself. The simplest extension is obviously the amplification of his own voice and, using the same system, adding music or other sounds of the world. A second way to extend himself is by using projected visuals on one or multiple screens. A third possible extension may be the use of television projected on a screen. This possibility will not be dealt with in this book as it is beyond the range of most churches in cost and usefulness.

Individual congregations may find any break with tradition painful. Start in a small way at a special time of the church year such as Christmas. People generally expect something unusual in worship at these festival seasons. If your first presentation is too elaborate, the coordination will be difficult. There will probably be some technical breakdowns or other distractions which may cause the people to reject the use of electronic media before it has a chance for success. In _every_ case a full rehearsal is necessary before a presentation is made. It is also easier to plan around a Christmas theme (when more visuals are available) than for any other season of the year. There is also a wide variety of good music and other sounds to be recorded and brought into worship.

The architecture of a building often makes it difficult to be very innovative in worship. By.careful preparation of a congregation and by creative use of sight and sound, some very significant worship experiences can be made mutually satisfying and challenging.

The steps in preparing a congregation for multi-media worship, the "hardware" necessary to achieve this sort of worship experience, and some practical suggestions for worship services based on experience will be discussed in the following pages.

CHAPTER I

The Church and Communication

The minister is the key to effective communication in an individual congregation. Every minister who is vitally concerned with the proclamation of the good news has had special training in the art of sermon preparation and delivery. In his homiletics training, advice has been given in understanding the nature of the message, the development of an orderly presentation of the message, and effective presentation techniques. When he slips into casual or careless preparation or presentation of the message, the effectiveness of the communication is diminished.

Each of us understands the quality of intimacy called "presence." A speaker seems to be in a personal conversation with you individually even though you may be a part of a large audience or congregation. The listener is not aware that a microphone and amplifying system are between him and the speaker. The speaker is simply using the amplifying system as an extension of himself, as the medium. In most cases a speaker is confined to certain locations and limited gestures because the microphones are in fixed positions. Consider the use of wireless microphones for all leaders of worship so that movement will not be restricted. Instead of raising one's voice to be heard, a conversational tone can be used and "presence" can be cultivated.

A minister needs to have good voice training to develop his potential as a speaker, just as an actor or singer needs training to develop latent talent. This training should be reviewed often by a voice coach so that the talents for good communication improve continually.

Mannerisms often get in the way of effective communication. We do not know when we are falling into bad habits. Some person should be able to help by pointing out these annoying distractions. Being able to see ourselves in action can be very disturbing at the time but very helpful over a period of time. Have you considered video-taping a worship service sometime so that you can see yourself in action?

Continued education through preaching and worship clinics at regular intervals in his life is essential if the minister is to remain an effective communicator.

While it is necessary for a minister to be an effective communicator in all that he says and does, he is also called to be innovative in worship.

Continual use of any form of communication, no matter how stimulating, can be very deadening after a time. Variety is imperative to keep people interested. Each message of significance needs to be considered as to the most effective manner of presentation. The media form needs to

be considered. Should this truth be illustrated with an
object lesson? Should it be introduced in a special way
with some sound effect? Should it reach a conclusion with
a special visual or sound effect? These are the types of
questions that should be asked. Should this be presented as
a dialogue, a panel discussion, a role play, or another
media form? Could it be better presented in visual form?

Changes in worship will usually start with the
minister. In order to make the worship revelant, it is
imperative to bring the sights and sounds of the world back
into the sanctuary.

This blending of the world and worship can be done
with object lessons in children's sermons (the adults surely
get the point in this manner) and in adult communication.
Biblical stories and concepts are begging to be illustrated
with visuals and sounds.

Much of the music of the younger generation is very
provocative as it seeks to speak to the deepest frustrations
and longings of the youth of today. It would be well for
some of this music to be played for all to hear and then to
have a panel of young people discuss the theological issues
raised. The minister could be very effective as the modera-
tor of this panel (if he does not try to be authoritative).
Careful preparation would need to be made for this to be
spontaneous and yet well organized.

Many ministers "spring" a very involved and different worship experience on an unsuspecting congregation and
receive a very negative response to innovative worship.
Bringing in small changes and explaining them will cause
most congregations to respond favorably.

It is always a good idea to use very simple mechani-
cal innovations in the beginning, partly to acquaint the
people with the hardware of good multi-media worship and
partly to keep the minister from being more concerned with
the operation of machinery than with sincere communication.
The visual and the sound should be natural extensions of the
person leading the worship experience.

The creative nature of the minister can find real outlets as he begins to use some of the tools of the day which
are used in so many ways in the secular field of communication. It is important for the minister to see himself as a
coordinator of the communication process rather than as the
process itself. A wise minister also sees himself as the
coordinator of the worship experience which is produced by
a worship committee rather than by one man. He will be the
coordinator of the sound, visuals, and the action of worship.
He will also coordinate the work of the worship committee.

The worship committee should be able to plan and
produce as well as present the multi-media worship services
if it has informed and capable people among its membership.

Here are some possible additions to the committee that may be involved in the communication process.

A group of young people and adults who are very interested and knowledgeable concerning visuals and sound may add a whole new perspective to worship planning. There will need to be at least one technician to care for the equipment and make special electronic hookups. A handyman will be a real asset in construction of special screens and other physical properties. A person who can catalogue and systematize the many visual and sound resources will be an extremely valuable addition to the committee. All of these people working together can not only save the minister much time which he needs to spend in other areas of work of the congregation, but a new sharing of the meaning of worship will probably result to the advantage of the whole congregation. These people will be able to bring a perspective from the world which is often lacking in our worship. Including people and their talents in the worship of the church leads to enriching experiences for them and the entire congregation.

The worship committee will plan the worship experiences as a team. The insights gained from this common experience will be of significant value to the minister and the congregation.

The purposes of innovative worship may be defeated if there is too much emphasis on the unusual and on constant

15

change. It is not a good idea to force media forms so that
the intended meaning is lost. The visual image is very
strong, and if not used carefully may alter the worship experience considerably.

There will be many times when the minister may want
to produce and present a particular idea or sermon by himself. In this way the media become very direct extensions
of himself rather than of a committee or group.

The members of the committee will be constantly on
the alert for magazine or other pictures to be copied for
inclusion in future worship services. The visuals librarian
will be filing these pictures properly under meaningful
headings in a cabinet. When a particular worship service is
being planned, it will be easy to find just the right pictures to photograph. When you have at your disposal dozens
of pictures to choose from, you will have a better presentation than if you are trying to make the presentation fit
the visuals.

After you photograph the pictures, store them again
in their original place. In one series you may only want a
portion of the original picture, and in a later presentation
you may want another portion or the whole picture. The
visuals which have been made should be filed under the same
headings as the pictures so that cross-referencing can be
done easily. There is no one adequate system for filing

2" x 2" slides. There are many systems for filing them
under particular groupings. One good way to preserve certain
productions would be to leave them in trays ready for showing.
Another system is to file the slides in coin collectors'
plastic sheets and put them in notebooks. This filing system
will keep the slides clean, and twenty of them can be viewed
at one time by holding them up to a light source.

Overhead transparencies will also be filed under specific categories so they can be easily located by persons
who did not do the original filing. The content of overhead
transparencies will be covered in the second chapter.

After you have made the decision to develop the use
of sight and sound in worship and have a good working committee gathered around you, a regular working area needs to
be planned for and set aside for constant use. This room
should be large enough for your committee meetings and have
tables to work on and places for your slide viewer, copy
stand and other equipment which you will use. It will need
a good closet for storage of the equipment when it is not in
use. This closet needs to be under lock and key, with careful control of accessibility. The room should be free from
other uses so that a partially completed program can be left
on the sorting table. To ensure good sound production,
arrangements need to be made for a very quiet work room.

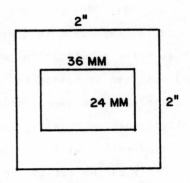

A. 135 SLIDE FORMAT

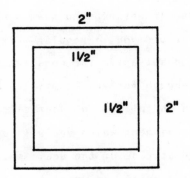

B. 127-620-120 SLIDE FORMAT

FIG. I. SLIDE FORMAT

CHAPTER II

Production of Visuals

There are several different types of visuals common-
ly used in multi-media presentations. We will consider
them in the order of their usefulness in an integrated
multi-media presentation.

2" x 2" SLIDE VISUALS

The most useful visual is the 2" x 2" slide.

There are two common sizes of transparencies used in
2" x 2" slide mounts. The most common is the 135 mm mount
which has dimensions as shown in Figure 1-A. The mount is
designed to hold the transparency produced by processing
your 135 mm slide camera film. The other common mount is
the 127-620-120 film size and has dimensions as shown in
Figure 1-B. This mount is particularly useful for non-
camera techniques in slide production, which will be covered
later in this chapter.

The slide mounts are available in cardboard and in
plastic. Some new plastic mounts are now coming on the market which are almost as inexpensive as the cardboard mounts.
They are reusable and thus a real money saver.

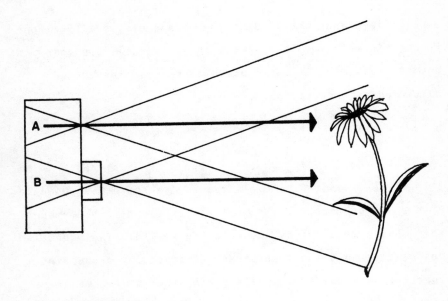

A. VIEWFINDER   IMAGE
B. LENS   OR   PICTURE   IMAGE

FIG. 2. PARALLAX

Cardboard mounts are superior in that the transparency is firmly in place and not "sloppy" as in the plastic mounts. This is particularly true when certain portions of a visual are masked for one reason or another.

Slide mounts are also available in special designs, such as heart, diamond, star, oval, and flower petal, which may be used for special effects.

Plastic mounts will not get dog-eared in use. Bent slides and frayed corners are the two main causes of slides jamming in a projector. Incidentally, if you clip about 1/8" from each corner of your cardboard-mounted slides, you will prevent most jamming in projection. Use a fingernail clipper or sharp, heavy scissors or a razor blade.

You may have a 135 mm twin-lens reflex or other external viewfinder camera that allows you to produce acceptable slides. You are encouraged to use this camera to the limit of its potential. There is one problem that all such cameras have in closeup work. This is called the parallax effect. Briefly stated, you see a different perspective of the image in your viewfinder than the lens sees and records on the film. Figure 2 will help to explain this.

Obviously, if you frame your picture as the viewfinder sees it, you will cut off the top of the image and you will be disappointed with the results. You can learn some

21

special techniques of tilting the camera to make allowances for this problem, but it is still a guessing game at best. This problem becomes more acute in closeup work and in the use of your camera on a copy stand. You may not be able to see any of the picture to be copied at extreme close range. A copy stand is a framework allowing you to photograph objects or images at extremely close range under artificial lights. This piece of equipment is very useful and will be explained in detail later in this chapter.

Another item missing on twin-lens and viewfinder cameras is the built-in light meter. You will need a light meter to get correct exposure readings in critical photographic situations, and it is essential for copy stand work.

Ingenious photographers who know their cameras can take some exceptional pictures with their twin-lens reflex or viewfinder cameras. You may be one of them! If you are having any problems in your closeup photography, it would be a good idea to find a specialist in cameras who can advise you in purchasing some of the necessary equipment to do all of the work you would like to do with your present camera.

There are so many different cameras, each with its own special problems, that it would be impossible to cover all cases in this manual. Your camera specialist will be happy to share your joys and frustrations in photography. A good camera specialist is more interested in solving problems than in selling equipment.

KODAK "INSTAMATIC" CAMERA

Many people have an "Instamatic" camera and would like to use it more extensively in slide production. It is possible to do this by purchasing the "Visualmaker" accessories to use with the camera. These accessories include 3" x 3" and 8" x 8" copy stands that compensate for the parallax problem, which we have already explained, and also for the problem of correct lighting and focusing, which will be explained under the SLR camera section which follows.

The slides come out with a viewing area approximately 1" square. The film size is 126. It is usually a cartridge which simply slips into place in the camera.

There are many different qualities of these cameras, depending on the price range. They all have the same basic body size and will work on the "Visualmaker." The better quality camera obviously will have better lenses.

There are some advantages to using this type of camera for copy work as well as for outdoor photography:

1. It is simple to operate. When the camera is in place on the stand, it is no more complicated to operate than snapping pictures out-of-doors, as the focusing is

23

preset, the lighting is automatic with the flashbulbs or cubes, and the framing is done by proper positioning of the stand on the object or picture to be photographed. A child can operate the camera with very limited instruction.

2. It can now be used for quite a bit of relatively closeup photography out-of-doors as well. It has the necessary closeup lenses built into the stand.

There are, however, several disadvantages to this camera and the "Visualmaker." It is not recommended that you buy this equipment if you are serious about doing good visual production for multi-media presentations.

1. There are very few square pictures in magazines or other places where copying is done. Also, many objects or pictures smaller than 3" need to be photographed. In such cases a lot of masking of the picture or masking of the slide after it is produced is necessary.

2. The "Instamatic" is relatively expensive to operate, since the cost of flashbulbs or cubes must be included with each picture. The film ordinarily is not available in bulk, so film costs remain constant.

3. The quality of the visuals cannot match the quality of visuals produced by cameras whose lenses alone cost more than the whole "Instamatic" camera.

4. The lack of versatility in future use is a drawback to the purchase of this equipment. The camera cannot

24

be adapted for use with telephoto or extreme closeup lenses.

SLR CAMERA

There is only one sure way to eliminate the problems we have been sharing, and this is to own a good single-lens reflex camera with a through-the-lens light meter. The rest of this manual will take for granted that you have this type of camera.

There are several reasons for the purchase of the type of camera and equipment which will be recommended: (a) You can see exactly the picture you are taking, since you are using the same lens for viewing and taking the picture. (b) Since the light meter is an integral part of the viewfinder, you can get the correct exposure without an extra light meter except in the most intricate lighting. (c) You can use the same basic camera for just about anything you may want to do later.

In the purchase and operation of a camera, you will be constantly referring to f-stops. An f-stop is a manner of controlling the amount of light coming through the lens opening. Each f-stop is double the previous stop. Most SLR cameras will have lenses ranging from f/1.8 and f/22. Remember that the largest opening is f/1.4 and the smallest opening is f/22. This chart may help you understand the differences.

f/1.4	Largest opening or most
2	light entering through
2.8	the lens.
4	
5.6	
8	
11	
16	
22	Smallest opening or least
	light entering through
	the lens.

Different lenses have maximum openings other than the full f-stops shown above. An f/3.5 lens allows one half more light than an f/4, and an f/1.8 allows one third more than an f/2.

The following basic equipment may be bought over a period of time as your interest and skill call for additional equipment. There is no need to buy equipment that will be unused. You can better use your money by taking more pictures with your present equipment.

When purchasing your SLR camera, be sure that it has a built-in light meter. The basic lens should be a 55 mm f/1.8 or f/2. A 55 mm lens is called a normal lens, as it records on film nearly the same image that the eye sees. Objects are not distorted and distances are in perspective. A short focal-length lens will exaggerate distances between objects. A long focal-length lens will compress distance and "flatten out" all space between the object photographed and the camera. The shutter speed will probably go up to

1/500 or even 1/1000 of a second. You will find that there
will be very rare circumstances that call for more than
f/1.8 in aperture (lens opening). You may want to spend
some extra money to get a Macro lens. This one lens can
focus from infinity to within an inch or so from the object
to be photographed. It will probably be no faster than f/3.5
or f/4, but its wide range of usefulness will be found in
copy work, which we will detail later in the chapter. At
the same time get a lens brush, cleaning fluid, and some
cleaning paper. A dirty lens can spoil many good pictures.
It would also be a good idea to get a gadget bag to keep your
film and other materials together. The only other suggestion
regarding the camera purchased is that it have a Pentax
threaded mount or a Canon bayonet-type mount for durability
and interchangeability of lenses. There are probably more
Pentax mount lenses of good quality available. You can
expect to pay well over $200 for a camera and this basic
equipment.

Your camera specialist may have a good secondhand
camera that will save you a lot of money. If he stands behind it, count your blessings and buy it.

TRIPOD

A very important item in photography is a good tripod for closeup work and time exposure. Be sure that the

head comes off and can be suspended underneath for closeup shots at ground level. You will also need a cable release for time exposure and telephoto lens use as well as for slow speed photography. You can expect to pay over $30 for a good tripod.

FILTERS

Two filters are recommended for your 55 mm lens. You will want a polarizing screen and a conversion filter (FLD) to convert daylight film for use under fluorescent lights. The fluorescent lights are for copy work and will be explained later in this chapter.

A polarizing filter (or screen) is not actually a filter but rather a screen that allows only the light rays that come in one direction to enter the lens. Light "vibrates" in all directions at right angles to the light ray itself. By allowing only the vibrations from one direction to enter the lens, the contrast of an image can be changed considerably. Blue skies become much bluer, the contrast of clouds and sky is much sharper, and reflections are reduced. In addition, foliage is much greener and more vivid in color. Pictures take on a professional look.

If you do not have an SLR camera, you will have to make allowances on exposure, as filters cut out some of the available light. Your SLR camera will automatically tell

28

you the proper exposure if you have the ASA rating set
properly.

An explanation of the ASA rating of film may be
helpful at this point. ASA stands for American Standard
Association. All film has a rating related to the amount
of light necessary for proper exposure of the film. The
lower the ASA rating, the more light is needed for exposure.
You can get the necessary light by using either a larger lens
opening or a slower shutter speed or both.

STROBE LIGHTS

Strobe lights are essential for indoor photography
and very useful as back or fill lights in critical outdoor photography. Be sure that your strobe light has an
adjustment for use with wide-angle lenses. The strobe
light is basically "packaged daylight," so no change is
necessary when using outdoor film for indoor photography
with these lights. For the best indoor photography you
should have two lights. One will be used as a fill light
and the other as main light. One good strobe light with
rechargeable batteries will cost over $50, but you will find
it to be a very versatile piece of equipment. If you are
not going to do a lot of photography with strobe light, it
may be better to get a unit that uses batteries and AC
current but is not rechargeable. This will save you quite

29

a bit of money. With either of the units, if you set up
for much indoor photography, you can plug the flash into
any standard outlet. Do not make the mistake of buying a
cheap light and then having to trade it in at a loss for a
good light when you buy your wide-angle lens, which will be
recommended later in this section. You can use two strobe
lights for the copy stand and can use daylight film without
any filters. This will be explained later in this chapter
under copy stand work.

EXTENSION TUBE SET

If you do not have a Macro lens, an extension tube
set is essential for copy work and closeup photography.
A 55 mm normal lens cannot focus closer than about 18 inches.
When you want to get closer than that, you will need to use
extension tubes. You can do many things with the extension
tube set, including up to 1.17 magnification. A bellows
unit is essential for greater magnification, and you can also
add a slide copying attachment later. It is not advisable
to purchase closeup lenses, as any work to be done with them
can be done with the extension tubes or bellows.

EXTRA LENSES

Extra lenses may be bought when you have the money or
want to do some special photography. Here is a suggestion

30

for the purchase of additional lenses. (There is no agreement among camera specialists on this.) Buy lenses in a planned order, such as frequency of use. A 28 mm wide-angle lens is one of the most useful for indoor and outdoor photography. If you are going wide-angle, go to 28 mm rather than 35 mm. The 200 mm telephoto is the longest focal length that can be hand-held in a practical manner. The 85 and 90 mm are portrait lenses. This is a way to increase the focal length of these lenses by using either a 2x or 3x teleconverter. You can mentally figure the focal lengths of these lenses by multiplying each lens by 2 or 3. When using the teleconverters, a good bit of resolution is lost and it is much more critical to focus. If picture quality is not critical, you can save a considerable amount of money by using the teleconverter.

Do not discount the value of a good zoom lens to replace the 85 and the 200 mm, as it can be good from 70 to 235 mm, depending on the brand. A zoom lens is heavier to handle than a comparable telephoto lens and is thus difficult to use in crowded conditions. It also has a much slower speed overall to make it usable at the longer focal length. Generally the longer the focal length, the slower the speed of the lens.

Do not rule out buying used lenses and lenses made by other manufacturers. Many of these name brand lenses are

31

very good and are precisely engineered to fit your camera.
Vivitar, Soligor, and Lentar are some lens manufacturers.

It might be of interest to you to know the differences in the angle of view of various lenses. This chart should help.

Lens	Angle View in °
20 mm wide-angle	95
28 mm wide-angle	74
35 mm wide-angle	63
55 mm normal	43
85 mm mid-range portrait	28
105 mm mid-range	23
135 mm mid-range	18
200 mm telephoto	12
300 mm telephoto	8
400 mm telephoto	6
500 mm telephoto	5
600 mm telephoto	4
800 mm telephoto	3
1000 mm telephoto	2

These are approximations. Brand name lenses will vary
slightly from this chart.

FILM

You are going to need film for your camera. There is
a confusing number of brands of film on the market. Many
of these can be used for slide production. Each one has a
different ASA rating, which we have already explained.

Eastman Kodak has the widest range of film stock as
well as more outlets for purchase and facilities for processing than any other company. Let us take a look at film

Production of Visuals

in the order of preference for slide production.

1. Ektachrome X is a very popular film with an adequate speed (ASA 64) for most photography. It can be used
indoors with filters. The colors are good and no problem
in shutter speed for most photography.

2. High Speed Ektachrome daylight film is rated
ASA 160 and thus is especially good for fast action with
telephoto lenses and for other circumstances where speed is
essential. This film can be shot at speeds up to ASA 640
but requires special processing when "pushed" above the
normal ASA 160. This speed would give you light for almost
anything you might want to photograph. Such fast speed
decreases color quality, but it may be the only way to get
a desired effect.

Both Ektachrome X and High Speed Ektachrome may be
processed using a kit and process E-4. This process takes
one hour in the laboratory and requires very accurate water
temperature control. In order to make this economically
feasible, you would have to develop a minimum of six rolls
per week. Kodak laboratory processing is highly recommended.

Kodachrome X, with the ASA rating of 64, has rich
color and is very popular for slide-making. The speed is
adequate for most photography.

Kodachrome II daylight film is rather slow (ASA 25)
for some occasions in photography. The colors are rich,

33

and this film is preferred by some very good professional photographers.

All Kodachrome film must be processed in commerical laboratories.

There are some other films such as Kodachrome II Indoor and High Speed Ektachrome type B indoor film which can be used under photo flood conditions without filters but must have filters to be exposed in daylight. It is recommended that you stay with daylight film and use strobes for indoor light and filters for copy work for best overall results.

Experimentation is necessary in photography so that you may find just the film and just the process to get a desired effect.

Many professional photographers use only one film in all of their picture-taking. There is real merit in this, as they know what their camera and film can do in any given situation and thus they can concentrate on framing and composition while the camera simply becomes an extension of their eyes.

Your pictures should steadily improve in quality and content as you become more familiar with your camera and lighting conditions. Your camera specialist will help you analyze your pictures and will give some tips for better pictures in the future.

34

Now that you understand the workings of your camera and are very familiar with its capabilities, it is time to try some new things with some of that equipment you purchased.

COPY STAND WORK

Many times there are beautiful pictures in magazines or art books that you would like to use in a slide presentation. Be very careful in the use of pictures that you copy from magazines or books, as they are generally copyrighted and use of them without permission of the copyright holder may lead to a lawsuit.

You can copy pictures and many other things very easily with your SLR camera. You can copy some things very well by putting them out on a flat surface or on a wall and using daylight for illumination. You will take these simply as outdoor or daylight pictures. When you find that the picture or object is not large enough to photograph with your 55 mm lens, it is time to bring out the extension tube set.

When you want to move indoors and photograph pictures, you will need a copy stand. Buy this stand without lights and use either fluorescent or strobe lights rather than photo flood lamps. All lights have a color temperature, and this varies with the voltage to the lamp. In order to

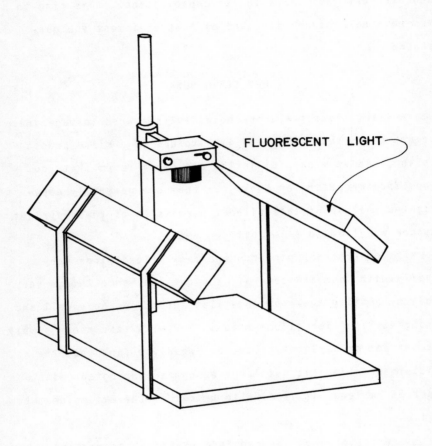

FIG. 3. COPY STAND

get a very accurate color temperature such as 3200K or
3400K, a voltage regulator will be necessary. The most
dependable light for accurate color temperature will be the
strobe light. You may want to use two strobe lights set at
45° angles to the table below the camera, as shown in Figure 3. You will need to do some experimentation on lens
opening and shutter speed, and you will need to cover the
lights with a white handkerchief to reduce glare.

If the colors are not absolutely critical, you can
use two double-bulb 20-watt fluorescent lamps and daylight
bulbs set at 45° angles to the table as shown. With an FLD
filter you can use daylight film and get very acceptable
results. It is much cooler and less tiring to work with
these lights than to use photo flood lamps. Always use a
shutter speed less than 1/60 of a second to avoid the
cycling of the lamps.

You will want to sort your pictures to be copied so
that the largest picture is first and they get progressively
smaller. Place the material to be copied on the table under
the camera with a piece of non-glare glass on top to hold
the material flat and also to aid in eliminating glare from
the lights. If your picture is large and you are copying
only a part of the original, you do not need to bother about
a border. If you have a small picture or object or want to
cut out a part of the original picture, you can do this by

masking with colored construction paper or other material for the desired effect. Experimentation is the name of the game in this work:

If you have a Macro lens, you will be able to do almost all of your copy stand work without adjustments or additions. As we have mentioned before, this lens is expensive and rather slow (f/3.5 or f/4), but speed is not critical under copy stand lights.

If you do not have a Macro lens, you can use the 55 mm lens down to a certain size picture and then you will need to add the shortest part of your extension tube set for smaller pictures. After this you will use the second longest tube of your set. When the pictures are very small you will need to use the longest part of your set. With some experimentation you can even photograph objects or pictures and magnify them slightly on your slides. A bellows can magnify a great deal more, and it can also be used with a slide copying attachment to make duplicate slides.

In all of this photography you will use your cable release to avoid moving the camera while tripping the shutter. The proper exposure will be shown in the viewfinder of your camera.

MATERIALS FOR COPYING

Portions of the Scriptures can be copied and used in

many ways to enhance worship. Make a special mask on the
back of a small piece of non-glare glass no larger than the
page you are copying. This mask should have an opening no
wider than the column of the Bible you are copying from.
The height of the opening should be adjustable for the
length of the verse to be copied. To make this mask adjustable, insert another piece of the same color paper
between the glass an'd the larger mask.

Christmas cards are beautiful and can be copied to
add a real dimension to special Christmas programs.

Stewardship quotations and portions of the Scriptures
having to do with stewardship can be typed specially and
then photographed. Different styles of type can be used
for varied effects.

Hymns and prayers as well as contemporary songs can
be copied and used for congregational use. Instead of the
people burying themselves in bulletins, they can lift their
heads and respond or sing out. Once again be careful about
copyright violations.

Great religious art can be reproduced on slides in
this way and shown in many circumstances to enhance worship.

In all typing, be sure that you have a good, clear
type for photographing. Remember that it is magnified
many times in projection.

A special process which can give some very unusual

effects may be of interest to you. Type material with a good black type on light blue or light red paper. Using Ektachrome X film and setting the ASA at 125 rather than at 64, you can photograph the material in the usual way. You now must have it specially processed as negative, with process C-22, and mounted as color slides. The colors will come out complementary; the printing will be white.

NON-PHOTOGRAPHIC TECHNIQUES

Clear vinyl with adhesive backing, such as "Marvalon," is a very valuable material in slide production. It is used as a backing in the production of various non-photographic visuals.

Regular mimeograph stencils produced by A. B. Dick come in two shades of blue, two shades of green, and in orange. Gestetner produces a yellow stencil in addition to the blue and green. Using a 127 slide mount as a guide for size, you can draw, type, or letter in the usual manner on the stencil. Be sure that none of the guidelines on the stencil is included in your visual, as these lines will show up in projection. Now by taking two 1 and 3/4" square pieces of "Marvalon" and putting one on the back side of the stencil over the image and another over the front side of the image, you are ready to follow directions on the box of mounts and mount as any regular transparency. The visuals produced in this manner can be very pleasing as well as unusual. They are also very inexpensive.

Another process using "Marvalon" has been of interest to many young people. It is called the "lift" process. You need to be warned at the beginning that the visuals produced in this manner are not of good quality, and also that the visuals should come out of discarded magazines, as the magazines will have to be cut up in the process.

By searching through magazines, particularly trade journals with good quality pictures, you can find pictures small enough to fit inside a 127 slide mount viewing area. Cut pieces of "Marvalon" into 1 and 3/4" squares, as in the previous process, and after peeling the backing off, rub the adhesive surface smoothly over the picture in the magazine. Be sure that you do not crease the vinyl or damage it in any way. Now cut the picture from the magazine and place it in a bowl of water. When it has soaked for a few minutes, the paper will slip off and leave the image on the sticky side of the vinyl. There will be a chalky material which will need to be washed off. You can carefully work this off with your fingers. When it is clear, put the visual aside to dry. Do not wipe it with anything, as it is sticky and will pick up lint or paper which will then be projected as part of the visual. When the first piece of vinyl is dry, add another piece of vinyl, sticky sides facing each other. Be sure that there are no air bubbles trapped between them. Now trim the visual to fit the mount by using the guide enclosed in the box of slide mounts. Follow instructions for mounting that are given on the box.

Overhead projector transparency material makes good slide material when you use various pens and liquids to make the impressions. You can mount this material as you would ordinary transparencies and draw or write on the material with overhead-projector pens, felt-tip pens, stencil correction fluid, stencil cement, fingernail polish, and white "Liquid Paper." The "Liquid Paper" is opaque and comes out true black in projection. India ink can also be used, and since it is opaque it comes out a true black when projected.

Acetate sheets in 20" x 50" size come in red, green, blue, and yellow as well as clear, and can be used the same as overhead projector transparency material for slide production. The colors are very pleasing as background for drawings in black.

Another process for producing slides in a non-photographic manner is called the thermographic process. The materials are shown by the brand name "Escotherm." Instructions are different for each type of paper purchased, so it is necessary to follow the directions which are enclosed in the package. The same basic techniques for producing over-

head transparencies are employed, keeping the visual size
to fit the slide mounts.

16 mm FILM

16 mm film is a very useful visual form in multi-
media.

Films are available to churches at no cost from many
sources. Some of these films deal with current problems
and can be incorporated into a multi-media presentation with
great effect.

Check with the film library operated by your denomi-
nation. Many films can be found that would be most helpful.
Some have rental fees and some are free.

Check with your local television station and secure
copies of outdated ads, which are generally 16 mm. By
careful editing and splicing, some very creative things can
be done. Remember that the sound track on sound films is
26 frames ahead of the visual frame.

Many film companies have footage that is not used in
final film productions, and these "out cuts" are generally
discarded. Often "out cuts" are very useful as segments in
multi-media productions.

16 mm film production is generally out of reach
financially and equipment-wise for any individual church.
The value of 16 mm film is in volume use. But by ingenious

43

and creative use of available film, some very significant
additions to multi-media productions can be made.

SUPER 8 FILM

If you have an 8 mm camera and have taken a lot of
film that would be useful in a multi-media presentation you
are planning, feel free to go ahead with the production and
use of this film. However, Super 8 film has nearly replaced
the regular film because the image it produces is approximately 50% larger and new techniques of adding sound to the
pictures have been more adequately developed.

Modern Super 8 cameras are a marvel of ingenuity.
Most of the problems associated with light and f-stops are
cared for automatically. For example, the light is automatically metered, and the lens adjusts for the proper
exposure. As long as your viewfinder meter says that you
have adequate light, you can take pictures safely indoors
with floodlights or out-of-doors with daylight. The film
is designed for 3200K flood lamps, so when you put on your
indoor light, a pin slips into place to move the filter out
of the way for indoor photography. When you are filming
out-of-doors, the filter is naturally in place to compensate
for the light.

Most of the Super 8 cameras have a coordinated focusing system and a zoom lens. When you first set the subject

distance in the viewfinder, in the manner prescribed by the
camera manufacturer, you set the lens for that distance,
and you are ready to take pictures.

There is no parallax problem since the viewing is
through the lens as in an SLR camera.

The modern Super 8 camera has a motor-driven mechanism that eliminates any spring winding for film advance.
The film is in a cartridge that simply slips into place and
requires no threading or other alignment.

Only quite expensive Super 8 cameras have the feature
of single-frame exposure. This feature opens innumerable
photographic possibilities and may be worth the extra
investment.

Kodachrome II film with an ASA rating of 40 is the
film used in most photography of this nature. There is a
new Ektachrome ASA 160 film which is used in circumstances
where the light is limited. The film must be processed in
a commerical laboratory.

The instructions which come with your camera are
very important and should be read carefully before you try
it out. You can practice without film to get the feel of
the equipment, so that movement and framing of the picture
become smooth and natural.

When you are ready to film a sequence, insert the
film cartridge and try taking the pictures. Remember that

you have a moving camera, so record action and not just still-life shots. Your SLR camera is best for still photos!

OVERHEAD PROJECTOR TRANSPARENCIES

It is possible to use large lettering, drawing, or cartooning with an overhead projector. Several overlays can be made to show progressive development of an idea or object. These overlays can be in different colors to clearly distinguish parts from each other.

Each overlay can be drawn or made with different colors of transparency pens. After the art work is done, the surface is sprayed with a clear acrylic to prevent any smearing of the surface.

Using 1/4" type on a special typewriter and using a heat process to make transparencies, some very good things can be done. Prayers, words to hymns, and other worship aids can be made up for permanent use. The heat process varies with each type of paper used, so follow carefully the instructions that come with the materials.

A complete system of transparency production has been developed by a company known as Escotherm.

It is possible to actually draw or letter on the material while the media show is progressing. This effect of immediacy can be very creative and meaningful in certain circumstances. It is also possible to point out specific

46

items on the original transparency while it is being shown,
rather than using a pointer on the screen.

FILMSTRIPS

Filmstrips are available on almost any religious
subject. Most denominational headquarters have a library
of popular filmstrips. Many of these visual aids can be
incorporated into a multi-media show with good effect.

The image is generally very clear, as it is large
in relation to the film. It is one half as large as that
of a 135 slide. Filmstrips are produced by using a one-
half frame 135 mm camera. They can be made by any photographer who has access to a one-half frame camera. By carefully photographing a sequence so that it has no pictures
out of order and by processing in the usual manner, you have
a filmstrip. It is not possible to edit a strip or replace
a picture as with slides.

There are many damaged filmstrips which are discarded
by companies or denominational filmstrip libraries. In such
a filmstrip there may be many individual pictures which are
not damaged. These can be cut out and mounted in special
2" x 2" slide mounts and shown as slides in a regular projector. With careful editing and use, some very creative
things can be presented.

Use of imagination in visual sources will lead you

to many other good ideas. Remember that experimentation
is the standard practice.

CHAPTER III

Sound Production

Sound is both a physical action and a psychological
sensation. Sounds may vary from very simple to very complex,
from very soft to very loud, and from very low in frequency
to very high. Sound recording and playback equipment must
be able to adjust easily to these varations in order to
produce good sound. Good sound is probably more important
than good visuals in carrying a message adequately. For
this reason, extreme care must be taken in all sound production and presentation.

TAPE RECORDERS

The basic part of a tape deck or recorder is called
the transport system. It includes the drive mechanism which
propels the tape from one reel, past the heads and onto
another reel. A tape deck may include recording and playback heads but does not contain built-in speakers. It is
used in conjunction with other component units in sound
production and presentation. A self-contained tape recorder
has recording and playback heads and a built-in speaker
system.

As mentioned earlier, you will need to find a sound

specialist as you found a camera specialist. This person
should be able to advise you on equipment purchasing and
provide you with good maintenance and repair service.

Plan all purchases so that you will have an integrated sound system when completed. An integrated sound
system provides for all amplified sound to come from one
source. It will include a good amplifying system with all
microphones and tape or record sources fed into it, and will
have speakers which present good, clean sound in the room.

REEL-TO-REEL TAPE RECORDERS

A reel-to-reel tape recorder is recommended for versatility. This is particularly helpful when it is necessary
to edit tape.

Tape recorders generally will have three speeds.
They are 7 and 1/2, 3 and 3/4, and 1 and 7/8 inches per
second (ips). Some unusual recorders also have 15/16 inches
per second. For recording music and any other sounds that
go above 13,000 H_z, the 7 and 1/2 speed should be used.
3 and 3/4 ips should be used for speech and certain music
that does not go above 12,000 or 13,000 H_z. Some machines
can reach near 15,000 H_z with the 3 and 3/4 ips speed. The
1 and 7/8 and 15/16 speeds should be used for speaking only.
The speed must be adequately controlled to reduce "wow" and
flutter. "Wow" is repetitive slow variation in tape speed,

and flutter is high-speed variation in tape speed. They should not exceed .09% at 7 and 1/2 ips for good sound production and presentation. The wow and flutter variation will be more pronounced at lower tape speeds. For this reason it is best to use faster tape speed whenever possible.

It may be desirable to have an 8-track continuous-loop recorder to provide some long-play possibilities. When the tape comes to the end, it automatically reverses itself and records or plays back to the beginning.

A good tape recorder will have three heads. This feature allows monitoring of the recording as it is being made. In this way you can make any needed adjustments or corrections at the time of the recording. With the three-head machine it is also possible to have features such as echo effect, sound with sound, and sound on sound.

It is almost imperative to have a stereo recorder so that you have the potential of controlling slide projectors on one channel while a sound track is recorded on the other. Music and other sound effects in stereo take on a different dimension which may be well worth the difference in amplifier cost. You may even consider a quadrasonic system so that you will have two channels for synchronized slide projector operation later.

An instant stop or pause control will be of significant value when using other equipment in mixing sound and

51

in editing. When the recorder is not monitored continuously,
an automatic shutoff is of value because it will stop the
machine if the tape ends or breaks.

The tape recorder should have low impedance inputs
for recording. This allows the use of long microphone cords
and high quality microphones.

Accurate VU meters are essential to achieve accurate
recording. This is the only way to know the level of recording so that distortion can be avoided.

An outlet for using headphones is very convenient
for monitoring while recording, and for precise location
of sound in editing.

CASSETTE RECORDERS

Cassette recorders do not operate at more than
3 and 3/4 ips and thus are not able to record at more than
15,000 H_z. They generally operate at 1 and 7/8 ips, which
is only good for voice recording. They do not ordinarily
have three heads and thus are not as versatile in monitoring the recording or in doing special things like sound
with sound, sound on sound, or echo effects. Access to the
recording head is generally difficult, and thus precise
editing of the tape becomes a problem.

TAPE RECORDER CARE

It is essential to demagnetize the tape heads regularly. This should be done before any critical recording is begun. Regular cleaning of the heads with the recommended cleaning solution will remove the loose oxide particles which, if left on the heads, become abrasive. Dust particles also accumulate and will create static and other unwanted sound.

It is good to check tape speed regularly to be sure that recordings made at one speed will not be too slow or too fast if played back at proper speed. A recording made at too high a speed will be lower pitched when played back at the proper speed. A recording made at a slower speed will be higher in pitch when played back at the correct speed.

Regular maintenance and oiling as recommended by the manufacturer will keep your machine operating at peak efficiency for a long time.

TAPE

The tape used in recording is critical for good sound production. Quality tape is generally 1 and 1/2 mil in thickness. It may be one mil in thickness. The author recommends·202 Scotch brand tape for master recordings. A good general purpose tape is 175 Scotch brand. Tape should be polyester rather than acetate. Acetate breaks too easily.

53

Some people use one or even one-half mil tape in recording. The thinner tape sacrifices in several ways including: (a) easier breakage, (b) stretching, and (c) print-through of sound. A stretched tape will affect sound just as machine speed does. A break in the tape can usually be repaired with little noticable effect, but stretched tape must be replaced.

As the tape base is wound layer on layer on the tape reel, it acts as a cushion between the layers of magnetized oxide particles. If this layer is too thin, the sound from one layer may come through as unwanted sound to prior- or later-recorded material.

It is imperative that the recording level be kept below the maximum to avoid distortion and excessive print-through and that it be kept at a high enough level so that tape noise and other unwanted sounds are not recorded out of proportion to the wanted sound.

High heat and high humidity conditions after recording also increase the tendency for stretching of tape and print-though. Warping of the tape also results from these conditions. Tape should always be stored at room temperature and normal humidity. It is also essential that the tape be stored away from other magnetic fields such as electric motors or power lines.

MICROPHONES

A microphone is an instrument that translates sound
waves into electrical impulses. It must be of good quality
in order to maintain strong links in the chain of sound production. Microphones are rated on their ability to trans-
late faithfully these sound waves into electrical signals.
A tape recorder with a range up to 20,000 H_z is not necessary when your microphone may only produce signals up to
10,000 H_z. There are many situations in which such a microphone would be adequate, but it would be better to have one
that is capable of a wider range of sound.

The microphones that come with better quality tape
recorders may be of adequate quality for fair voice production, but almost all of them fall short when recording
music. You will need to buy separate microphones to do
quality sound production.

Good quality microphones are low impedance in nature,
so that long cords may be used. This is necessary to keep
the tape recorder away from the source of the sound and
also hidden from observation. Low impedance microphones
generally are 600 ohms or less in output, and high impedance
microphones may go as high as 50,000 ohms. Good quality
tape recorders are designed to use low impedance microphones.

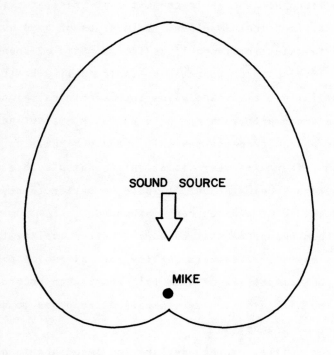

FIG. 4.

CARDIOID PATTERN IN MICROPHONE

There are several types of microphones available.
The best general purpose microphones are dynamic. They work
on the principle of a diaphragm with a coil in a magnetic
field. Electrical impulses are created as sound waves
activate the diaphragm. These microphones are capable of
reproducing frequencies up to about 18,000 H_z. This type of
microphone may be quite inexpensive or may be very sophis-
ticated and cost several hundred dollars. Dynamic microphones are basically omnidirectional but may be designed
to have a particular pickup pattern. The most used pickup pattern is the cardioid or heart-shaped pattern shown in
Figure 4.

This pattern may be much longer and narrower when
it is designed for long-distance directional use. Many
dynamic microphones are very durable and can withstand extreme abuse. Most microphones used in commerical sound
production are of this type. Many better quality tape
recorders come with dynamic microphones as standard equipment.

Another type is the ribbon microphone. Ribbon microphones have a very thin piece of metal suspended between
poles of a permanent magnet, much like a rubber band suspended between your fingers. As the waves of sound activate
the ribbon, electrical impulses are created and then trans-
ferred as with other microphones. These microphones are

57

able to reproduce a wide range of sound, but they are very
sensitive to shock and air movement, so they are limited
to studio use. They are used in recording studios because
of their extreme sensitivity and high quality. These microphones can also be made directional in their pickup pattern.

Condensor microphones work on the principle of a
very thin piece of metallic substance being near but not
touching a metal plate forming what is now called a capacitor. These microphones need a special high charge of DC
voltage to activate the capacitor. They formerly had a
special generator to provide this voltage but now have a
system whereby a small self-contained battery provides the
voltage for many hundreds of hours. They have been lowered
in cost now so that they are competitive with other good
microphones. They are very sensitive to sound waves and
thus have a good frequency response.

The crystal microphone is the least expensive and
the least responsive. It is so named because of a small
piece of crystal or ceramic which is bent or twisted and
produces electrical impulses in the process. These microphones cannot reproduce very good bass tones and cannot
faithfully reproduce tones over about 7,000 or 9,000 H_z.
They are high impedance in nature and need special trans-
formers to be used with low impedance tape recorders. Good
quality microphones of this type can be found, but most are

inexpensive and come with inexpensive recorders. They are
omnidirectional in nature and thus cause some problems for
good recording.

TURNTABLES

A turntable is a machine with a revolving disc which
turns at a fixed speed. The standard speed now is 33 and 1/3
rpm. Other speeds are 45 rpm for some "pop" records and
the old standard speed of 78. Some turntables also have
16 rpm, which some children's records use.

At the present time, quality turntables generally
come only with the 45 and 33 and 1/3 speeds combined.

Constant speed is maintained by the use of heavy
flywheels and synchronous motors. As in a tape recorder,
the variations in speed of a turntable will affect the
sound produced. Speed can be checked by using a simple
little disc on the turntable and shining a special light on
it. The lines on the disc will stand still if the speed
is right. They will go backward if the turntable is slow
and forward if it is fast. The disc will cost less than $1.
Most turntables have fixed speeds. Some very expensive ones
have adjustments for speed regulation.

In addition to constant speed, the tone arm is
critical to a good turntable. For good sound it must be
adjustable so that the weight of the needle on the record

is kept at a minimum. The tracking weight on modern records
should not exceed five grams. Generally speaking, two or
three grams will be sufficient. Heavy tracking will cause
excessive wear on both the record and the needle. The tone
arm should track at nearly the same angle to the grooves
from the outside to the inside of the record. There are
some elaborate systems on the market which seek to make
tracking very accurate.

Affixed to the end of the tone arm is a cartridge
which actually picks up the sound variations in the record
as a microphone does with live sound. A good cartridge is
a very good investment. Some will have two distinct pickup heads, one for 33 and 1/3 and 45 rpm records, and the
other for 78 rpm records. These should not be used inter-
changeably. Most good cartridges are designed for long-
playing records only. Since you will be using only 33 and
1/3 and 45 rpm records, one cartridge is sufficient. If
you do not use the preamplifier aspect of an amplifying
system, it is possible to use adapter cords with your magnetic cartridge and plug directly into the microphone inputs
of a tape recorder. A stronger signal and thus better sound
will be coming to the tape heads by using a preamplifier and
coming in through the auxiliary inputs.

It is best not to have an automatic changer mechanism
for the turntable. The automatic changer will be in the way

60

for most of your work, and it is best not to stack records
on top of each other. An automatic changer on a good turntable will cost quite a bit more money.

MIXING EQUIPMENT

In order to blend sounds and to combine live sounds
with recorded sounds in a smooth manner, it will be necessary
to work with some mixing equipment. Sony makes a fine, inexpensive mixer which can combine three or more sources.
It will also be a good idea to have a second tape recorder
to use simply for playback purposes. By combining the mixer
and the extra tape recorder with your turntable, it is possible to do almost any combining of sound you may desire or
need. The mixer allows smooth fade-in of music or other
sounds and is extremely valuable for this reason.

RECORDING HINTS

In recording it is necessary to observe some rules in
order to have a good product when completed. When recording
a live performance, observe these simple rules:

1. Mike each performer separately, if possible. If
this is not possible, you must mike each singer or group of
singers separately from accompanying musical instruments.
A singer does not reach the decibel level of a musical
instrument, and therefore his microphone level must be set

higher to balance the performance. It is best to use two
microphones in recording a soloist, even for a monaural
sound. By balancing two microphones, a better quality is
assured. The microphone should be placed so that the performer is singing or playing over the top of the microphone.
In this way some of the harsh sound is balanced out. High
frequencies tend to go in a more or less straight line, and
low frequencies seem to radiate. If high frequencies are
blocked off, they are either absorbed or reflected.

    2. To record a piano, it is best to record the upper
range with one microphone and use another microphone for the
lower range. A third microphone is often used in the middle
for balance. By putting two microphones into right and left
channels of stereo, a very fine stereo recording can be made.
The piano is one of the hardest instruments to record because
of the sharp peaks of sound it produces and the almost im-
mediate disappearance of the sound. Good microphones and
very sensitive recording heads are essential for good fidelity. It is very important to set these microphones to pick
up the sound from the strings of the piano rather than the
sounds from key movement and fingering.

    3. Microphones should not be placed in a direct line
in front of an instrument or a soloist in extremely loud
passages. It is best to turn the head or instrument about
10° to one side at this time. A balance between the softest

62

and loudest parts of the performance should be known ahead of time so that the recording level can be preset for as nearly accurate range of the sound as is possible.

4. Open-air recording calls for special precautions. Wind or any air movement may be very distracting. By using wind screens over microphones and turning directional microphones away from the wind, much unwanted sound can be eliminated. Dynamic microphones are probably the best for this type of recording situation. A ribbon microphone is too sensitive for outdoor use. When recording it is always essential to watch the VU meter to prevent distortion caused by recording at too high a level.

When recording from records it is important to follow several rules: (1) Keep the turntable covered at all times when not in use. This will keep dust from accumulating on it. (2) Be sure that there is no foreign material on the needle to cause unwanted sound. (3) Clean all records in a thorough manner using some good anti-static solution and a soft brush. (4) Keep the records clean by storing them away from dust and static conditions. (5) Do not allow your fingertips to touch any grooves.

When recording from a television or radio receiver, use direct connections rather than from speaker to microphone. This will prevent unwanted sound from becoming a part of your recording. It will also improve the quality

63

of your work, as the speakers on most television sets are not
of very high caliber. All television sound is monaural.
Most of it will not be over 4500 H_z, as this is the highest
frequency that can be transmitted over telephone lines. When
you are recording high fidelity stereo, the range may actually go to nearer 20,000 H_z if all equipment from the studio
to your receiver is in the best condition.

After gathering sounds from many sources, you can now
use your mixer along with the turntable and extra tape recorder to produce the finished tape.

Careful editing of unwanted portions can be done by
precise timing and noting of each individual section of the
tape on a note page. Your instant stop becomes very handy
at this time. Play the tape to the beginning of the unwanted passage and stop the recorder instantly. Now carefully
mark this location with a felt-tip or grease pen on the
shiny side of the tape. On most recorders you can bypass
the capstan and roller and leave the tape against the playback head. By moving the tape back and forth over the head
you can determine the exact spot where the deletion should
be made. After marking this spot, let the tape play until
you find the end of the unwanted portion. Do the same thing
here and, using a tape splicer, cut out the unwanted portion
and make a neat splice on the shiny side of the tape. If
you do not have a splicer, cut the tape at 45° angles to fit

back together. Put a piece of commercial splicing tape on
the shiny side of the tape and trim the sides so that the
splice is slightly narrower than the regular tape. This
allows a smooth flow of the tape through the guides and an
even flow from one reel to the other. Do not use cellophane
tape. If you plan to edit the tape, leave some extra space
between each performance or interview. Also be sure that
all segments of the tape are recorded at the same speed and
same sound level. Leader tape is very important on a completed recording, just as a cover is essential to protect
a book.

CHAPTER IV

Presentation of Sight and Sound

Each visual form has certain characteristics which make a distinct contribution to a multi-media presentation. Let us consider each one in turn and see what dimension it adds.

2 x 2 SLIDES

The major advantage of this visual form is that of being easily arranged for almost any kind of production. Slides can be sorted and put in any order and, if necessary for visual effect, can be reversed by simply turning them around. Damaged slide mounts can be replaced, and the transparency can be used again. To use rear projection screens, one simply reverses the slides in the projection tray.

Another feature of this visual is the clarity of the image. The image can be projected onto very large screens and still be very clear. Because of their size slides can be easily edited or sorted, and they can be seen without magnification in most circumstances. Words should be readable on the slide without magnification if they are to be read on the screen by the viewer.

It is possible to draw or letter on the original

slide if the work is done carefully. Each line or object is magnified many times. There are so many different ways to produce slides and also so many slides available for purchase on many subjects that their availability is almost unlimited.

There is one major weakness of this type of visual, and that is the lack of movement. Some effects simulating movement can be achieved by using a polarizing screen in conjunction with the projector and by using dissolve units, which are discussed later in this chapter. These units can create a dramatic impact by making it appear as though one image comes out of another or goes into another.

16 mm FILM

16 mm film is readily available on a greater number of subjects. Films on a wide range of subjects are available to churches from many sources, some at no cost, and others for nominal rental fees.

The size of the image is good on film. When projected, the image can be very clearly seen and understood. One great feature of 16 mm film is the movement which slides lack. Colors can be very vivid and natural. Sound, especially speech, synchronized with movement can be a very valuable asset. This is one of the strong features of this type of visual.

Editing of sound film must be done with great care,

as the sound is 26 frames ahead of the visual. Most sound
film when completed must remain intact. Splicing must be
very carefully done to avoid damaging the visual as a whole.

Production of 16 mm film is very expensive, but many
sources of this visual can be located, which will allow some
very creative multi-media material.

SUPER 8 FILM

Some members of your congregation may have Super 8
cameras and be willing to use their talents in filming
sequences for multi-media productions for worship. This
makes the visual form accessible on a wide variety of subjects. This film will not have sound synchronized on it in
most circumstances.

Movement can be photographed in a natural way. Film
can record many significant events in the life and work of
a congregation. Sights of the world can be brought into
worship through this type of visual. Editing of Super 8
film is not as complicated as that of 16 mm, since a sound
track is not involved.

A single-frame sequence showing a concept step-by-
step can be very strong visually. It can show progress
more effectively than slides can.

The quality is not as good as 16 mm film because of
the smaller size of visual. When Super 8 film is magnified

in projection to the size of 16 mm film or 2 x 2 slides, the grain of the film becomes apparent. It still can have a great impact emotionally.

It is expensive to incorporate sound with Super 8 film, and this probably would not be economically feasible for most church multi-media presentations.

OVERHEAD PROJECTION VISUALS

Overhead projector transparencies are actually large slides, but it is possible to write or draw concepts much more easily on these than on slides. Original art work can be done on the transparency rather than having to photograph it as with 2 x 2 slides.

Since the image is large on the transparency, it is very clear when projected. Successive layers of transparencies can depict the development of an idea or the progression of a concept.

Overhead transparencies are very versatile. They can be predesigned and then projected, or they can actually be produced as the presentation is in progress.

It is best to have a screen for use with the overhead projector alone. The projector will be in the line of the light beam of other projection equipment. It is necessary to turn the overhead projector off while changing transparencies since there is no shutter to move into place

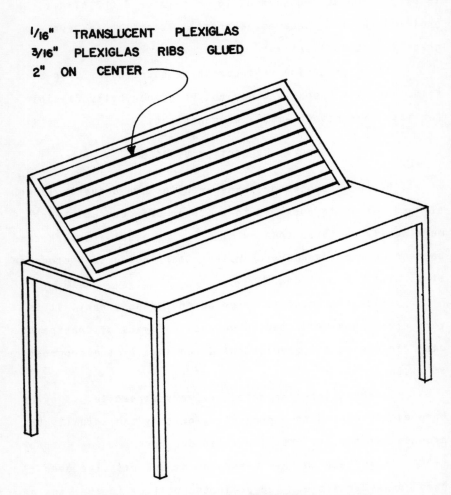

1/16" TRANSLUCENT PLEXIGLAS
3/16" PLEXIGLAS RIBS GLUED
2" ON CENTER

FIG. 5. SLIDE SORTING TABLE

70

between the light source and the transparency. This will
avoid the distraction of changing visuals. When a transparency is being made during a program, it may be better to
leave the light on the whole time. The immediacy of form-
ation of the transparency may be very strong visually and
detract from the other parts of the media project.

FILMSTRIPS

One of the best features of filmstrips is that they
are available on many subjects. Their size is also very
good for projection. In essence, a filmstrip is a series
of small transparencies. They cannot be changed in sequence.
Many filmstrips tell a complete story, and used in the midst
of other visuals can take on more importance or value than
when used alone.

PREPARATION FOR PRESENTING VISUALS

We have discussed the production of slides and other
visuals in a previous chapter. Now we come to the question
of editing the visuals and sorting and putting them in order
to tell the story which you have in mind. You will need a
large viewing-sorting table. There are many simple viewing
panels that hold 40 to 60 slides, but these are not large
enough to allow any real arrangement of slides. There is
an illustration of a slide sorter which holds 160 slides in

71

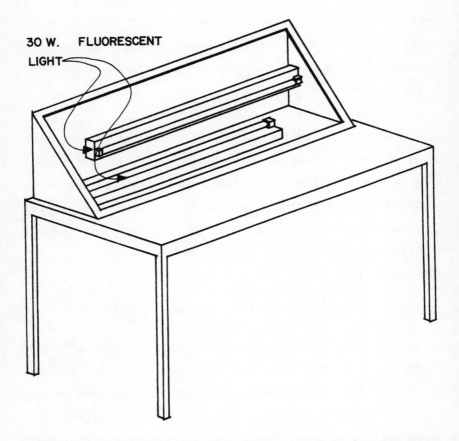

30 W. FLUORESCENT LIGHT

FIG. 6. SLIDE SORTING TABLE (DETAIL)

Figure 5. It has two three-foot fluorescent single-light fixtures mounted in back of the viewing area. One lamp is on the floor and the other is mounted on the back of the viewing area as shown in the illustration.

The viewing surface is 1/16" plexiglas with 3/16" plexiglas ribs glued 2" on center. These ribs hold the slides in place, as they sit at 45° angles to the tabletop. A working space is left in front of the viewing area for note-taking and other work.

If a larger table is desired, the size of the plexi-glas top can be increased. If it were set at a 60° angle, the viewing of the top slides could be made easier. A good handyman can build the frame and a plastics company can design the viewing screen.

Another good viewing table may be made by using a recessed ceiling fluorescent fixture which already has the plexiglas surface on which the slide support bars can be glued. This whole fixture then can be set up on a table against a wall. You can have a fixture either 30" or 48" long by 12" or 24" wide.

Fluorescent lights will not show the colors of your slides accurately in relation to projected color, but since all slides will be seen in relation to each other and you are primarily interested in viewing relationships, this is no particular problem.

73

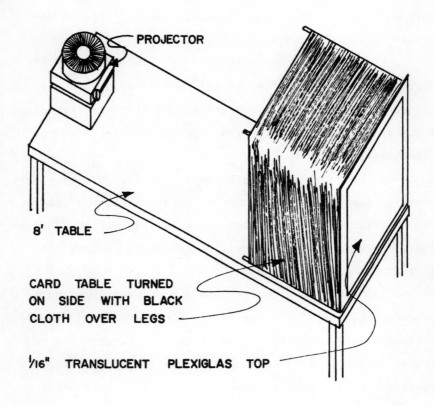

PROJECTOR

8' TABLE

CARD TABLE TURNED
ON SIDE WITH BLACK
CLOTH OVER LEGS

1/16" TRANSLUCENT PLEXIGLAS TOP

FIG. 7.
TABLETOP REAR PROJECTION SCREEN

If you are interested in exact color temperature in all stages of projection and presentation, some very expensive tables may be built or purchased that include incandescent lighting and fan cooling to remove the heat. Special fluorescent fixtures with adjusted color temperature for accurate viewing may also be bought.

It is recommended that you wear white cotton gloves while working with your slides and film. This is especially important when mounting slides. This will eliminate fingerprints and other foreign material which might detract from the clear viewing of your visuals. These gloves can be purchased at your camera store.

A secondary slide-sorting table may be made by cutting the top out of a card table, putting a 1/16" plexiglas sheet over the top, and taping the edges with some duct tape. By clamping a simple floodlight on one of the legs so that the light shines up from under the table, you can sort slides and group them as you choose. It will be harder to lean over the table, but it will be satisfactory unless you have a great number of slides.

Other uses for this tabletop screen will be found. For instance, it can be used as a rear projection screen in a classroom or in a convention setting. (See Figure 7.) If you drape some black cloth over the legs, the screen can be used in a well lighted room with good effect.

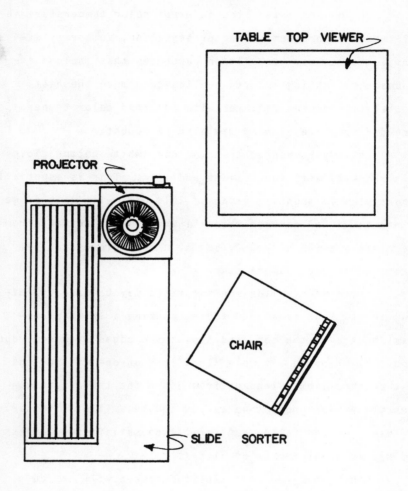

SCREEN

TABLE TOP VIEWER

PROJECTOR

CHAIR

SLIDE SORTER

FIG. 8. ROOM ARRANGEMENT

You can also use this screen to set up your projector and photograph an image for duplicate slides. (Be
sure that your projector lenses are clean and your slide
is clean!) To do this you simply photograph the picture
which is projected. You will not need any other lighting
You will need to set your camera on a tripod and use the
cable release because you will probably have a rather slow
shutter speed.

When sorting slides it is a good idea to have a projector beside you so that you can see what some slides look
like when projected. A screen should be in a convenient
location so that all this can be done without too much moving around. A good arrangement is suggested in Figure 8.

In addition to the slide viewer, you need a magnify-
ing glass to view certain portions of slides and also to
use while editing 16 mm and 8 mm film. You may invest in
an editor-splicer for the latter, but if you do not have
occasion to work with these visuals you may only need the
splicers.

PROJECTORS

Projectors for 2" x 2" slides are available in many
different designs and with many different features. They
may be as simple as an attachment to a filmstrip projector
or as complex as the automatic models used in professional

productions. Special conditions may require arc lighting sources, but we will discuss the projectors that will be useful in most churches.

First of all we will need to consider basic types. The preferred type is the flat rotary machine which allows the slides to fall into place by gravity force. It has a circular tray which holds 80 to 140 slides in order. Kodak and GAF are examples of this type. These projectors are the simplest to operate and the least likely to give trouble. There are more Kodak Carousel projectors around than any other kind. The Kodak projectors hold the slides in place with a movable floor in the tray and a ring on the top of the tray. The floor must be in the proper position when- ever the tray is removed from the projector, or the slides may fall out. The ring on the top needs to be in place as well. The GAF projectors hold the slides in place by small spring clips which allow the slides to fall into the pro- jection chamber when released.

A distinct advantage of the flat rotary projector is found when stacking slides on top of each other for multi- media presentations using one screen. The distance between projector lenses in a vertical position can be critical at close range. This is particularly true when you are using a dissolve unit and want one picture to replace another at the same spot on the screen. Accuracy in alignment of the slides in the projection chamber is also very important in the use of dissolve units.

A second popular type of rotary projector has the tray of slides set at a 90° angle to the base, as in the Honeywell or Sawyer's. All of these projectors have some sort of moving arm which pushes or pulls the slide into place for projection and then returns it to the tray.

A third projector type uses a cube or tray with the slides in line behind each other. Air Equipt and Bell and Howell are examples. This type of projector cannot be used for continuous showing, since the cube or tray must be reinserted at the beginning of each showing.

Another factor to consider is the ease of advancing or reversing the slides. The Kodak Carousel projectors have a forward and reverse button to activate, and in one second will either go forward or backward as you choose. The GAF and Sawyer's projectors have a cycle button which must be activated to change the motion from forward to reverse and back to forward.

LENSES

Projectors have a variety of lenses available for use under varying conditions. Most standard lenses come as 3- 4- 5- and 6-inch focal lengths. The 3-inch lens will project a larger image than the 6-inch lens at the same

79

distance from the screen. The longer the distance from the screen, the brighter the lamp must be to give a clear image. Another standard lens is the 4-6 zoom. This one lens will replace the 4- 5- and 6-inch lenses.

If you need a short throw to the screen because of limited space either in front of or behind the screen (which we will consider shortly), you may need a 2 and 1/2 or even a 2-inch lens. There are even 1-inch lenses made, but the cost is so great that we will not spend time considering their use in normal projection circumstances.

A 7-inch lens has been made available by Kodak for long-distance projection. If you go beyond this distance you will need special light sources for projection and also special lenses. This equipment will be necessary in some churches, but the use of rear projection screens may solve some of the light problems and also will get the equipment out of the way of the congregation.

Some projectors have only manual focusing of the lenses. Others can be focused by remote control and some focus automatically after the first slide has been focused correctly. Modern projectors have a focusing system which is fast and smooth. The focusing is hardly noticeable when viewing the presentation. Some older projectors took a second or more to focus properly.

It may be a good idea to have two automatic-focusing

projectors for use with your dissolve unit. The extra projectors need not be automatic-focusing.

Most projectors now use a quartz Halogen lamp as the
source of light for projection. This type of lamp lasts
much longer than the old incandescent lamps and remains constant in light output for the life of the lamp.

Simplicity of operation, ease of maintenance, and
general availability for rental or borrowing are all factors
to be considered in the brand of projector to purchase.

16 mm PROJECTORS

The basic operation of 16 mm projectors has remained
constant for many years. Advances in lamps, in quieter
operation, and in the automatic threading of film make modern
projectors very desirable. It is possible to stop for individual viewing of a frame and to single-frame some projectors. Some have variable speed, while others only have
constant speed.

If a film is shown by rear projection, you will need
to use a mirror to reverse the image and thus make the picture come out right from the viewing side. This is true
for all film projection. All sound on film is monaural, and
the image is in a 3 high to 4 wide ratio.

SUPER 8 PROJECTORS

Super 8 projectors ordinarily do not include sound
on the film. A recording strip can be placed on the side
of Super 8 film, and with special recording equipment the
sound can be synchronized with the film for later showing.
Many home projectors have inadequate light sources for
presenting a large picture image.

OVERHEAD PROJECTORS

An overhead projector is a very simple piece of
equipment. It can be quite useful in worship. There is
one disadvantage to it, and that is the necessity of its being set up very close to the screen for projection. The
focal length of the lens does not allow moving back from
the screen in order to become unobtrusive. This difficulty
can be resolved by the use of a rear projection screen, which
we will consider later in this chapter. A mirror will be
needed to project the image from behind a screen if you are
drawing or using a line production. If you are using ready-
made transparencies, it will only be necessary to reverse
the visual on the projection table.

FILMSTRIP PROJECTORS

Many filmstrip projectors have an inadequate light

source to project a clear image except in extreme darkness.
Projecting a large image also calls for more light than
some projectors can produce.

If a filmstrip cannot be reversed in showing, a
mirror will be necessary for rear screen projection. Additional focal length is often necessary to make a filmstrip projector compatible with 2 x 2 slides.

SCREENS

Screens may already be built into your sanctuary!
A smooth wall surface in the right place can be just right
if painted white with a flat latex paint. If you are not
this fortunate in your building, you will need to plan some
sort of screen for presenting visuals.

Screen size is important for best viewing. A simple
rule to follow for best viewing is to have the first row of
seats at least two screen-widths back from the screen and
the last row not more than six screen-widths back. A room
in which the last row of seats is 90 feet from the screen
should have a screen 15 feet square.

FRONT PROJECTION SCREENS

Front projection screens will need to be placed so
that all people can view the image with ease and clarity.
The surface of the screen is of significance. A matte white

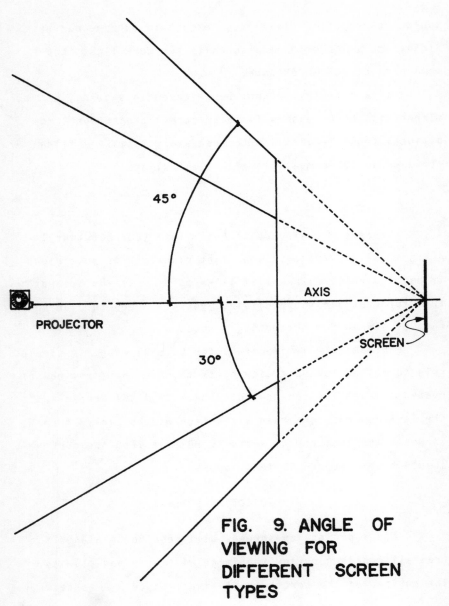

PROJECTOR

45°

30°

AXIS

SCREEN

FIG. 9. ANGLE OF VIEWING FOR DIFFERENT SCREEN TYPES

surface is the least expensive and can be viewed from a
wider angle. Figure 9 will help to explain this.

If a room is wide in relation to its depth, so that
people will be viewing from more than a 30⁰ angle from the
axis of projection, a matte white screen is almost imperative. With this screen surface, some loss of image bright-
ness will occur when the room cannot be darkened adequately
during daylight hours.

If the room is longer and narrower, you can use
beaded or lenticular surfaces for better daylight showing.
With either of these types, the viewers must be seated
within a 30⁰ angle on either side of the projection axis.

There is another screen now on the market that is
called "stereo black." This screen can be used with only
limited darkness. It has a covering of miniature fish
scales which reflect the light. If this screen is placed
high, it must be tilted out at the top so that the reflection from the projector comes to the viewers. Consider it
as you would a mirror in placement.

Scrim is another material which can be used as a
screen. This coarsely woven fabric is used in theaters
for many special effects and can be used effectively in
churches. When lights are on behind the scrim, it is
possible to see through it very easily. Objects behind the
scrim take on a veiled or shadowy quality. When projecting

on the material from the front, enough light is trapped in the fibers to produce a picture of about the quality of magazine printing. This material can be sprayed with polyvinyl acetate and made more translucent.

REAR PROJECTION SCREENS

Rear projection of pictures has opened many new perspectives in media use.

The simplest and cheapest screen material is a white plastic or vinyl shower curtain. This material can only make a 6' x 6' screen. There will be a "hot" spot in the middle where the projector light is strongest. You can eliminate this spot by hanging a "dodger," such as a quarter, about a foot in front of the projector in the light beam. Experimentation will give the best distance. This will diffuse the light and give you an acceptable projected image. Another material which comes in much larger sizes is the clear plastic used by building contractors. This material is usually too transparent and needs to be sprayed with some matte white latex paint to make it translucent and thus produce an acceptable image. You will need to experiment some on the texture needed. Most paint sprayed on this surface will flake off in time.

For regular use and for larger screens of professional quality, one would need to go to a material such as that

86

produced by Polacoat or DA-LITE screen companies. This
screen material can be used in daylight and it does not
have a "hot" spot. The colors in the transparency come
through very true, and the angle of view is not critical.
It is not possible to see through the screen, but light can
be projected and some very effective shadow effects can be
achieved in this manner.

Scrim may be sized with the polyvinyl acetate, or
unbleached muslin may be sized with this material and used
for rear projection. Any materials such as these have some
opaque fibers and reduce the quality of the image. In much
of our presentation of visuals, we are not focusing all of
our attention on the beauty and clarity of the picture but
on the general effect created. The screen in this case is
not so critical. If you are presenting art masterpieces
and want the congregation to get the visual impact of their
beauty, you would certainly look for a quality screen.

If you use rear projection screens, you will find
many times that there is not enough room behind the screen
to get an image sufficiently large without very expensive,
short (one- or two-inch) focal-length lenses. You can project into a mirror and from the mirror to the screen. In
this way you can almost double the image size in the same
distance. A mirror or prism is essential for showing film
in rear projection in order to put the image in correct
viewing relationship.

87

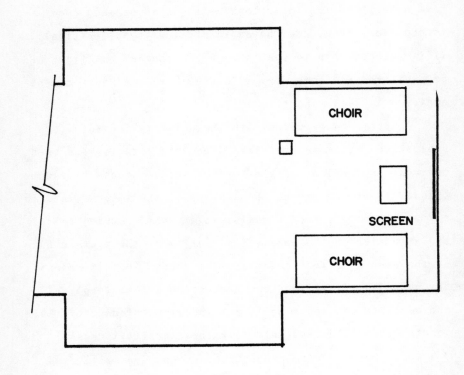

FIG. 10.
CHURCH WITH SCREEN BUILT INTO
FRONT WALL

A new material called "Refex" is now available. It
is a polyester film with an aluminum backing mounted on a
lightweight frame. It can be purchased in any size up to
48" x 144". The material can be easily cared for and does
not deteriorate.

Front surface mirrors are also good but are heavy
and will usually need a backing for mounting. Plate glass
mirrors may also be used for this purpose. A plate glass
mirror may produce a second image on the screen. This is
caused by one reflection from the surface of the glass
and a second image from the back of the glass where it is
silvered. There will be a slight loss of light with the
plate glass, but it is not noticeable due to the polyester
film on the Refex material.

SCREEN LOCATION

A serious question arises in the location of a screen
or screens in a church building. The most serious problem
occurs if the choir is behind the pulpit, facing the
congregation. It is almost impossible to set a screen
where both the choir and congregation may have equal viewing ability. If it is in a right relationship for one
group, it will be backward for the other. It may be possible to have a screen built in against the wall as in
Figure 10.

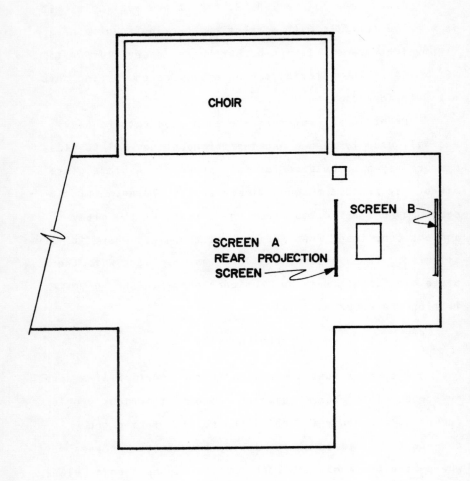

CHOIR

SCREEN B

SCREEN A
REAR PROJECTION
SCREEN

FIG. II.
CHURCH WITH TWO SCREEN VARIATIONS

The screen may be housed in a frame that will blend perfectly with the architecture and can be lowered by electric controls whenever it is needed. Usually this type of church would have this area illuminated by artificial lights which could be turned off and thus solve the light problem on the screen.

Other church buildings have quite similar design, with a variation like that shown opposite in Figure 11.

In this design all people are on the same side of a line from the pulpit to the wall in back of the communion table or altar. The screen may then be a scrim hung between the pulpit and font, as in A. It might also be a rear projection screen as in A, or it might have a screen against the wall as in B.

This building may have a balcony--an ideal location for projection. It is best to keep the electronic equipment out of sight as much as possible to avoid confusion and distraction.

In a church with a baptistry, the focal point is usually here. A screen may be mounted above this opening and lowered over it for viewing of visual images.

In some churches it is possible to locate a screen on a wall to the right or left of the pulpit.

If it is possible to build a screen into a wall and

have it covered with draw drapes when not needed, this
would be of great advantage.

It is a good idea to have a screen in view as a part
of the regular architectural lines so that it will not appear to be "movie" time at worship when it is used. If it
is left as a natural part of the building, people will become familiar with it and its use. There is no need for a
screen to be unused with the many possibilities for the use
of visuals which we will detail in the next chapter.

Ordinarily the projection of visuals calls for a
lower light level than is used in worship. Many modern
churches have eliminated as much window space as possible
to make it easier to air condition and to control sound.
For this reason the dimming or turning off of the artificial
lights will leave the room sufficiently dark for good visual
presentation. If your building is of older construction
and a great deal of light comes in, it may be necessary to
put some sort of shutters or blinds on some or all of the
windows. These may also be useful additions to the acoustical balance.

It is a good idea to have the control of room lights
and the control of the media equipment in one place and in
the hands of one person so that the presentation of sound
and visuals will be smooth and effective.

SOUND PRESENTATION

What is good sound? There are certain steps that
must be taken to present good sound after it has been produced properly.

A specialist must be consulted in this area as you
consulted a specialist in camera and in sound production.
Every link in the chain of sound production and presentation
must be strong for the worshiper to receive good sound.

Whether to present monaural or stereo sound is a
decision that must be made at this point. It is true that
a great deal of the sound which is presented will be monaural, but the beauty and clarity of stereo sound may be
worth the extra cost.

The amplifier is a vital link in the presentation of
good sound. It should have an adequate power output so that
it will not have to be used at the maximum volume setting.
When an amplifier is used at or near maximum gain or amplification potential, a distortion results, which is very un-
desirable. The amplifier should operate at a level where
distortion and unwanted sounds of the system itself are not
amplified. It should amplify all sounds in the spectrum
from high to low in a proper balance. A sound specialist
will tune the amplifier to fit the room and take other
factors into consideration to complete the installation.

The speakers are an essential link in the chain of
good sound presentation. Good sound cannot come from inadequate speakers. Speakers which may be perfect in one
building may not work at all properly in another. Speakers must first of all be able to handle the power output of
the amplifier. In the second place they must have a good
frequency response. In the third place they must adequately
distribute the sound to all parts of the room.

The directional nature of many speakers is probably
their biggest weakness. In certain parts of the room the
sound is louder than in others. Certain parts of the room
get more low sounds or more high ones. High sounds generally go in a straight line and low sounds generally are more
diffused. Proper speaker design and alignment by a reputa-
ble sound specialist will eliminate these problems. It is
a poor investment to get inadequate speakers when all other
links in the chain of sound presentation are strong.

Good sound is as free as possible of unwanted sound.
Unwanted sound may be street noise, air conditioning, air
movement, or sounds from an adjoining room or hallway. It
is possible to reduce the noise level coming from the outside by using tight-fitting windows and doors, wall insulation, and even some outside barriers such as walls and
shubbery. Installation of sound-absorptive materials on
the surfaces of inside walls will have little effect on

reducing the noise level in the room if sound is originating on the outside of the building. This sound will have to be reduced by wall insulation or a buffer such as shrubbery, a wall, or another building.

For internally produced sound such as air movement or movement of people, special work can be done to the air conditioning system or the aisles or corridors to reduce this unwanted noise.

The acceptable noise level in an empty church should not exceed 35 or 40 decibels. A level higher than this may be distracting to the worshipers.

Good sound must also be intelligible. We are now concerned with internal acoustics and sound control. At least 65% and preferably 80% of the speech sounds must be heard and understood for a room to be acoustically accepta-ble.

Sound must be loud enough to be heard. Average con-versation is at a level of approximately 65 decibels. This level of sound must be presented for good hearing in each part of a sanctuary. This level in a sanctuary may be reached only with an amplifying system, and if this system is not of good quality, the distortion may make speech unintelligible.

If a room has a long reverberation time, one sound may not have died out before another comes, and this may

cause the sound to be blurred. Too short a reverberation
time will call for a sound to be amplified more than necessary, as reverberation adds to the level of sound. Speech
needs a shorter reverberation time than music. Speech
should have a reverberation time of about 1.2 to 1.5 seconds, depending on the size of the room. Music should have
a reverberation time of 1.5 to 2 seconds. A balance must
be found between good acoustics for speech and good acoustics
for music. This balance will be from about 1.4 to 1.8 seconds reverberation time, depending on room size. With the
proper balance found and established by acoustical specialists, the proper volume and balance must be set on the
amplifying system for good sound presentation.

It would be well to consider having several microphone outlets around the room so that all sound may be
presented from one source even if people are participating
in worship from several places in the room. Cordless microphones are particularly good since they do not restrict the
movement of leaders or participants in worship.

Many sanctuaries are limited in the number and placement of electrical outlets. Arrangements need to be made
so that adequate power is available at the projection area.
Outlets should also be located around the room for various
uses in innovative worship.

SIGHT AND SOUND SYNCHRONIZATION

As stated earlier, multi-media is the blending or combining of two or more media forms into an integrated whole.

The simplest combining of sight and sound may be presenting a picture while the minister is preaching. Or it may be using one projector and synchronizing its operation with music as a prelude or meditation time. Speech may be added from a third source, such as a live voice, for a very strong reinforcement of the message.

A dissolve unit and two projectors using the same screen can produce some very dramatic effects to show similarities, differences, and progression of ideas as well as just beautiful images.

Dissolve units basically reduce the lamp voltage on one projector at the same time that the lamp voltage on another projector is being increased. In this manner one image simply dissolves into another.

These units vary in cost from about $200 for the simplest to over $500 for the more complex models. The rate of dissolve can be adjusted on some models.

It is also possible to synchronize the advancing of slides on one projector or one dissolve unit with signals put on one channel of a stereo tape recorder and the music

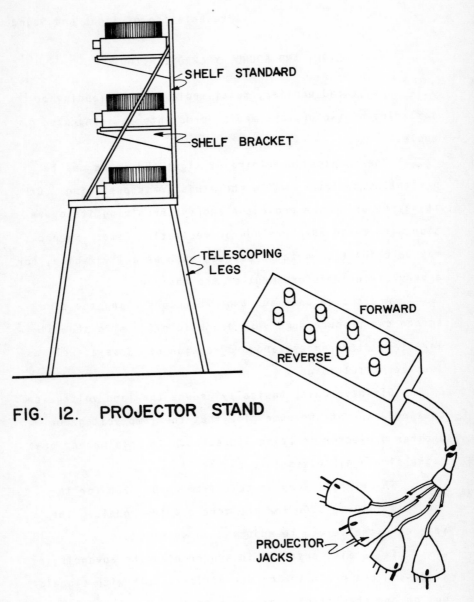

SHELF STANDARD

SHELF BRACKET

TELESCOPING
LEGS

FIG. 12.   PROJECTOR STAND

FORWARD

REVERSE

PROJECTOR
JACKS

FIG. 13
CENTRAL CONTROL UNIT
FOR FOUR PROJECTORS

or narration on the other channel. An inaudible sound is
put on the cue track of the tape recorder, and as the signals come along the tape, the slide projector is activated.
It is important to keep this track of the tape recorder out
of the circuit of the sound presented on the other track.
Do not record the cues at too high a level or some of the
cue sound may be picked up on the other track. More complicated synchronizers put these signals on several different sound frequencies or series of pulses. Only the right
frequency or number of pulses will actuate a particular projector. Since you will be using one channel for actuating
the projector or projectors, you will have monaural sound.

A relatively new arrival on the sound scene is the
quadrasonic system. This system has four speakers driven by
a special adapter on your stereo amplifier, or it may be
recorded on a four-channel deck which actually records four
independent channels instead of two as in stereo. It is
possible to record stereo on two channels and put cues on
the other two channels to activate two projectors or two
dissolve units in a synchronized whole.

A very dramatic effect can be achieved by the use of
three projectors on one screen. By projecting on the top
half with one projector and on the bottom half with another
projector, you can demonstrate contrasts, similarities, and
the progression of ideas. At certain points there will be a

major emphasis using the third projector to fill the whole screen with a large image. Whenever you want a projector to remain on and yet not show an image, simply insert a slide masked over with black photographic tape or a 2" x 2" square piece of cardboard in place of a slide. Any 2" x 2" slide that is not of projection quality is perfect to make into a black or blank slide.

These three projectors may all be stacked on one holder using different focal lengths on the lenses, as shown in Figure 12.

Using four-inch lenses on the upper and lower projectors and a three-inch or two-and-one-half-inch lens on the third projector, you can complete the setup. You will now need a central control unit to activate the three projectors in a simple manner.

Figure 13 is a diagram of a central control unit which is able to control four projectors with one unit rather than with four separate controls.

Using two of these units, it would be relatively easy to control up to eight projectors manually.

There are also many expensive and elaborate controls on the market. These may cost up to $1,000 or more and can perform as many as 80 or more functions in sequence. Some operate using 1/4" magnetic tape and some use punched tape.

It is a good idea to begin in a very simple way and

build up to more complicated media use as talent is developed and equipment is bought and mastered. There is a
real danger in trying too complicated a multi-media presentation at the beginning and making technical errors
which detract from the beauty and impact of the presentation. Always rehearse completely any multi-media presentation!

CHAPTER V

Architectural Considerations

Let us consider some ideal arrangements for innovative worship in a church. As plans are made to remodel
existing space, the ideal may be kept in mind and every
effort made to come as near as possible to this goal.
Any building must be carefully planned both for the present
and for the years ahead.

A church building should have all rooms serving
multiple purposes. Space should not be planned to stand
idle for five or six days a week anymore.

The sanctuary should be able to be varied in use
because every worship service is not identical in plan or
practice. It is a good use of money to plan for the same
room to be used for worship and fellowship. This room
should not be long and narrow. It should not be wider than
it is deep. A good relationship is three long and two wide.
In this way all of the people can sit near the action or
worship.

The seating should be movable with good chairs that
can be locked together when necessary for seating in rows.

These chairs will cost nearly as much as pews, but
they will be much more practical for multiple use. People

will not be trapped in certain locations and styles of
worship as with fixed seating. The pulpit furniture should
be movable so that different worship services can be planned
without being restricted in the location of the worship
center. It would be well to have a raised platform at the
end of the room opposite the main entrance so that many
different types of worship can take place with all people
able to see and participate more easily. The pulpit and
other furniture can be removed entirely for certain occasions in worship and fellowship.

A large rear projection screen three times as wide as
it is high should be built into the wall in back of the
raised platform. It should begin three feet above the
platform and continue as high as necessary for screen size
in relation to the room. A room 48 feet long will need a
screen 8 feet high. This screen area should have sliding
doors to protect the screen from damage when not in use.
The doors should be able to be opened for one, two, or three
screen widths, as necessary for the presentation.

Placing the screen in this manner allows it to be
used as a scenic background for religious drama taking
place on the platform and for backlighting actors who
would be silhouetted on the screen. These actors could be
in the projection room and lighted from behind by using the
projectors with either full white light, colored transparent

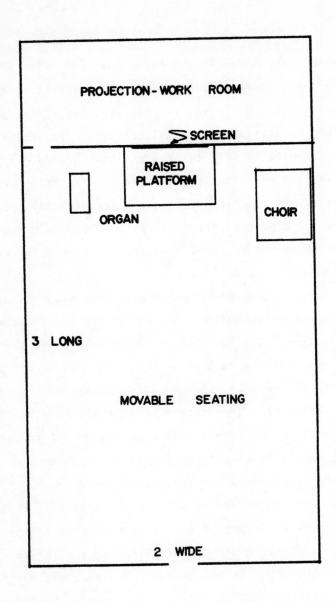

FIG. 14. IDEAL CHURCH DESIGN

slides, or slide mounts with different shaped openings. Some
very unusual effects could be developed in this way with
creative blending of drama and electronic media. (See
Figure 14.)

As we have just detailed, all projection equipment
would be located in the room directly behind the screen.
This room would be sufficiently large for all work to be
done on sight and sound editing and for storage of all
visuals and sound.

The sight and sound projection equipment would be
able to be controlled from the pulpit or from another location in the worship room. This master control location
should be so arranged that all parts of the worship room
can be seen, and the lighting controls would also be at
this location.

The choir and the organ console would be on opposite
sides of the platform and sitting at 90° angles to the
congregation. In this way all parts of the congregation
will be able to participate in all parts of the worship.

Electrical outlets would be placed around the room
and in the floor in the center of the room for convenience
in using the room for many purposes. Microphone outlets, if
needed, would be placed in the same manner so that individual participation from the congregation could be heard
easily.

The room would have a minimum of window space so
that air conditioning costs and noise level could be controlled more easily. Location of the building in relation
to traffic or other noise factors should be considered.

If plans are being made to remodel present facilities, some or most of these ideas can be incorporated into
such programs. It may be necessary to use front projection
with equipment and controls operating from a balcony. This
would limit some of the creative use of media, but not
eliminate it. Some very creative things are being done
with limited budgets. Be sure that you know what you want
to do before taking off into a major remodeling or building project. A good architect can put walls around and a
roof over almost any space that is needed. Do not let a
room restrict the innovative worship that is called for by
a pilgrim people today.

Appendixes

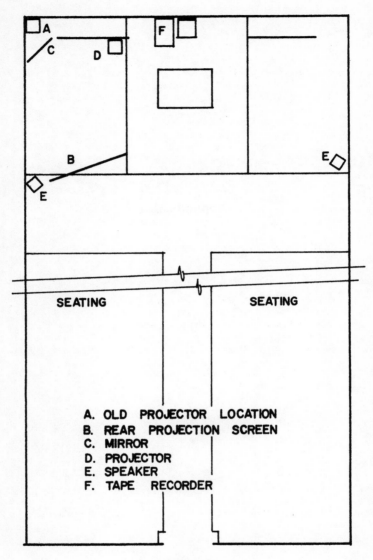

FIG. 15.

**FLOOR PLAN OF HYDE PARK
PRESBYTERIAN CHURCH**

APPENDIX A

The Hyde Park Church Experiment

A small congregation organized in 1910 in Austin,
Texas, was looking for a part-time supply pastor when the
author enrolled at the University of Texas to work on a
master's degree in radio, television, and film.

Most of the members of this congregation are over 60.
It has had a succession of supply pastors almost since its
founding. With the great number of ministers over the
years, much adaptability has developed. The church is in
a neighborhood changing from single-family homes to multiple-
family homes and apartment houses generally occupied by
university students. The congregation is blessed with
leaders who are willing to experiment.

The sanctuary is very simply designed and constructed,
and lends itself very easily to sight and sound presentation.
A floor plan is shown in Figure 15 to better demonstrate the
simple changes which were necessary.

The first use of multi-media was at a fellowship
supper when a simple two-projector, two-screen program was
shown. This program was based on the contrasting ideas of
greatness found in Matthew 18:1-4. A discussion of the idea
of illustrating sermons with pictures and other possible

109

uses of multi-media in worship interested several people
enough that they purchased some new and used equipment so
that we could do some experimenting. Following this presentation, several sermons were preached using object
lessons to illustrate the idea presented. Each of these
illustrated sermons was well received, and people began ask-
ing about plans for using pictures in worship. The ground-
work had been laid and the way cleared for regular use of
multi-media in worship.

As you will note in the floor plan of the sanctuary,
there are two walls on either side of the pulpit. They are
each five feet wide and go to the ceiling. Using each of
these walls as a projection screen, we presented the first
multi-media worship service. Pictures of the birth of
Christ were shown on the left wall, and the words of the
music were projected on the right wall when it was time to
sing appropriate carols. The narration of the program was
from the pulpit. In this manner the environment of worship
was controlled throughout the service, since the congregation did not need lights turned on for any part of the program. The worship closed with a candlelight service and
set the stage for bigger and better things.

Soon after this program was presented, a rear screen
projection system was installed using a shower curtain
and a projector set in the back corner of the church at

position A. The screen was placed at B with a framework
braced in place as a temporary installation. Later this
screen was replaced with a six-foot Polacoat screen and a
frame was suspended from the ceiling. This frame was designed to blend in with the surrounding materials and architectural lines. In order to increase the image size and
not have to buy a very expensive lens, the mirror arrangement was installed. The mirror is placed at a 45° angle at
C. The projector sits on a stand at D. This arrangement
is much better for several reasons. The projector controls
and the amplifier controls are both at this location. With
an ordinary remote control cord, the projector can be activated from anywhere in the pulpit area, even when the person with the control cord moves down to stand right beside
the screen for certain effects.

A turntable was used to play music through the amplifier system for some time until a new tape recorder was
purchased. Both the projector and the turntable were in
the back corner at A. Playing the music from the turntable
directly into the amplifier caused problems in editing music
smoothly and stopping at precisely the right time. When
this was all done behind the wall in the corner, it was
rather comical, as the minister would appear and disappear
to turn on and off the various pieces of equipment. When
all of this took place out in the open beside the pulpit,

it became obvious that the music was recorded, and some of
the effect was diminished. When the new tape recorder was
purchased, the music was edited in recording, and new
speakers were installed at locations E. The music now has
good stereo balance, as in a living room, and the recorder
is sitting on a low table at location F. It can be unob-
trusively controlled along with the slide projector for
maximum visual and sound effect. Most of the equipment is
owned by the author. Two slide projectors have been bought
by members of the congregation. Many different uses of
these pieces of equipment have been arranged outside of the
congregational use in the sanctuary. The rear projection
screen can be lifted out of its frame and folded up for
portability.

Each step that is taken in using multi-media worship
has been well received. There has been no negative response
by any person. Certain choices of visuals and sound have
been questioned, but when explained have been accepted. This
can be attributed to a very gracious congregation and to
careful preparation of the congregation for this type of
worship. Possibly the shortage of equipment and the simple
beginnings were a blessing in disguise. Whenever media
forms are not used in worship now, people express their
missing them.

APPENDIX B

Worship Ideas

Here are some of the actual uses we have made of
sight and sound in worship. Instead of and sometimes in
addition to the prelude played by the organist, the special
theme or setting of worship has been done by carefully se-
lected music and pictures. Sometimes one picture would be
shown, and at other times a series of pictures would be
shown while the music was being presented. Here are a few
of these relationships for an idea of the setting created.

```
Pictures:  Depicting mental anguish
Music:  Second movement of Mozart's 40th Symphony
Sermon:  "The Inadequacies of Life":  Romans 7

Picture:  "Ecce Homo" by Reni
Music:  Crucifixion spirituals played by the organist
Sermon:  "The Christian Life--A Life of Suffering"

Picture:  "Christ, the Universal Savior" by Hsu San Chun
Music:  "We Have Come to Worship God"--Hindi hymn
Sermon:  "The Universality of Christ"

Picture:  "The Last Supper" by Wood
Music:  "Come to the Banquet," sung by the Medical
        Mission Sisters
Sermon:  Communion:  "Fellowship and Breaking of Bread"

Picture:  Sunset--an original photograph
Music:  "The Spacious Firmament on High"
Sermon:  "The Heavens Are Telling":  Psalm 19
        contrasted with Romans 1:18-25

Pictures:  People in different walks of life
Music:  "He's Got the Whole World in His Hands"
Sermon:  "The Earth Is the Lord's":  Psalm 24
```

Visuals have been used as prayer guides. Prayer is thought of and taught as conversation with God. All language used in worship is current conversational English. Visuals of our need for confession such as scenes of pollution--industrial and private, of inhumanity to man, such as war, poverty, loneliness, and also of wastefulness and useless spending of money set the mood for confession. Other visuals have been used for prayers of intercession, including a series of space-exploration visuals on the Sunday that astronauts were walking on the moon. Visuals of previous moon landings were used. Visuals of government leaders are shown at times when we would remember those in authority over us. Visuals of world leaders have been shown as we pray for them. Visuals of almost any circumstance can be found in various magazines, and with a good selection committee and a good photographer at work, these visuals can be most informative and helpful. Recordings of people can be most effective here too. Prayer requests made by the sick and others who are unable to be present at worship could be brought to the attention of the worshiping congregation in this manner.

The possibilities for the use of multi-media in sermons are almost endless. The simplest use might be in putting the salient points of a sermon on the screen as they are presented orally. In addition, visuals just naturally illustrate certain truths, and they can be used to make a point clearer more easily than by using many words. Sermons may be introduced by using visuals for a setting or subject. Sound may be used as an introduction. Some popular songs of today, as they speak to social issues, lend themselves to commentary and analysis in a religious context. Great music of the ages also can serve as an introduction to sermons. Many hymns and anthems are Scripture portions set to music. The hymn "The Spacious Firmament on High" is based on a part of The Creation by Haydn, and this in turn is based on Psalm 19. Why not begin a sermon with a recording of this great hymn or the creation text and use slides depicting the beauty of the world for the first part? For contrast use Romans 1:18-25 and the need for special revelation as the second part. Psalm 46 ends on a prophetic note that God has already brought wars to an end and a new order has taken place. This great affirmation is at the heart of the Hallelujah chorus of The Messiah by Handel. Why not close a sermon on Psalm 46 with the Hallelujah chorus sung by a good choral group or your church choir, and have slides of the kingdoms of this world disappearing and a new order arising? No more commentary is necessary.

A sermon on the life of Christ, using slides taken of stained glass windows, can be very meaningful. Pictures of different settings of the cross and the crucifixion can

115

be most helpful. One beautiful stained glass window depicting the fulfillment of the law as portrayed by the Ten
Commandments is overshadowed by the cross, portraying the
gospel. This window speaks so clearly that any verbalizing
would be redundant. Simply showing the visual, reading
Matthew 5:17-20, and then having some moments of silence for
meditation would be a complete sermon.

When you begin to work with visuals and sounds in
worship, you will find that you will start to think in visual terms and that sounds that you have taken for granted
take on real significance. You become more alert to the
world that surrounds you, and you want to share this beautiful world with others. When you see the defacing of the
world by careless people, you also find a great desire to
change this for the better.

Another use of visuals in worship would be to put
the words to hymns and current songs on the screen so that
everybody can see them and sing out rather than have their
eyes glued on a page of a hymnbook or bulletin. There are
many popular songs that speak more clearly to this generation
than some of the hymns of years ago. In order to use these
songs in worship now, they either have to be memorized or
duplicated and bound into some sort of hymnbook. By the
use of large type on overhead projector transparencies,
these songs can be shown for easy viewing by the whole

congregation. While we are on the subject of overhead projectors and transparencies, how about projecting affirmations
of faith rather than printing them in a bulletin? Everyone
can stand, look straight ahead, and clearly affirm his faith.

Words to music on slides or transparencies are particularly good when you would like to control the environment of worship. When you are having worship by candlelight and do not want to alter the environment by turning
on the lights for congregational singing, project the words
of the hymns and let everyone participate freely.

Bibliography

Advanced Camera Techniques for 126 and 35 mm Cameras.
        Eastman Kodak Co., 1969.

        This booklet covers a great deal of very basic
        photography. The article on lenses is particu-
        larly good.

Adventures in Existing Light Photography. Eastman Kodak
        Co., First Printing 1971.

        This is an excellent booklet on film use with-
        out artificial lighting.

The Audio-Visual Equipment Directory. Fairfax, Virginia:
        National Audio-Visual Assn., Inc., 1972-73

        A quite complete listing of equipment for all types
        of media presentations.

Benson, Dennis C. Electric Liturgy. Richmond: John Knox
        Press, 1972.

        Benson shares innovative worship ideas and gives
        especially helpful suggestions about how to meet
        the needs and anticipate the responses of individual
        worshipers. Includes 2 LP's.

Bloy, Myron B., Jr. Multi-Media Worship. New York: Sea-
        bury Press, 1969.

        This is a rather interesting book dealing with
        innovative worship. Some of the viewpoints regard-
        ing worship are excellent.

Deves, Peter B. and Elliot N. Pinson The Speech Chain.
        Bell Telephone Laboratories, 1970.

        This is probably the most understandable introduc-
        tion to sound.

Fabun, Donald. The Dynamics of Change. Englewood Cliffs,
        New Jersey: Prentice-Hall, Inc., Third Printing,
        1968.

        A superb volume depicting the changes taking place

around us. A minister may get quite frustrated with the church after reading this book.

Feininger, Andreas. Successful Color Photography, 4th Edition. Englewood Cliffs, New Jersey: Prentice-Hall, Inc. 1968.

An excellent book if you really want to get into technical aspects of color photography. Much information is taken for granted.

Filters. Eastman Kodak Co., First Printing, 1967.

A very basic guide to filters for those who want to do more advanced photography.

The Fourth Here's How Techniques for Outstanding Pictures. Eastman Kodak Co., 1967.

The articles on slide duplication and producing a slide-tape talk show are worth the purchase price.

Howe, Reuel L. Partners in Preaching. New York: Seabury Press, Second Printing, 1967.

This book has some good suggestions on the general need for communication in worship.

Jansen, John Frederick. Let Us Worship God. Richmond, Virginia: The CLC Press, 1966.

A very basic book on the subject of worship. Particularly useful in advocating worship in all of life.

Kodak Films for the Amateur. Eastman Kodak Co., 1971.

This book has all that you want to know about film.

Ladefoged, Peter. Elements of Acoustic Phonetics. Chicago: University of Chicago Press, 7th impression, 1971.

An excellent introduction to sound and hearing.

McProud, C. G. All About High Fidelity and Stereo. Fort Worth, Texas: Allied Radio Shack.

This little book offers a rather good introduction

to high fidelity equipment and operation of this
equipment. It is a sequel to <u>Using Your Tape
Recorder</u>.

<u>More Here's How Techniques for Outstanding Pictures</u>.
Eastman Kodak Company, 1964.

This booklet is good for the two articles on
titling and lenses.

<u>New Adventures in Indoor Color Slides</u>. Eastman Kodak Co.,
First Printing, 1969.

This booklet is particularly good on using photo-
flood lamps for indoor pictures.

<u>Producing Slides and Filmstrips</u>. Eastman Kodak Co., First
Printing, 1969.

This booklet is worth the price for the section
on film.

Roberts,Richard. <u>Hi-Fi and Stereo.</u> London: Collier-
MacMillan, Ltd., 1965.

The section on sound is particularly good.

<u>The Seventh Here's How Techniques for Outstanding Pictures</u>.
Eastman Kodak Co., 1971.

The article on slide projection is worth the purchase price.

Smallman, Kirk. <u>Creative Film-Making</u>. New York: Collier
Books, 1969.

The best basic book on film making. It covers all
basic equipment and its use.

Stevens, Stanley Smith, Fred Warshofsky, and editors of
Life. <u>Sound and Hearing</u>. New York: Time-Life, Inc.,
1965.

A beautifully written book with many good illustrations to make sound and hearing understandable
to the average person.

The Third Here's How Techniques for Outstanding Pictures.
    Eastman Kodak Co., 1970.

    This booklet is particularly good for the article
    on "pushing" color film.

Using Your Tape Recorder. Chicago: Allied Radio Corpo-
    ration, 1969.

    This book gives a fairly complete introduction
    to sound and recording in non-technical language.
    A sequel to this book is All About High Fidelity
    and Stereo.

Van Bergeijk, Willem A.; John R. Pierce, and Edward E. David,
    Jr. Waves and the Ear. Garden City, New York:
    Anchor Books, Doubleday and Co., Inc., 1960.

    This little book is a good introduction to sound
    and hearing.

Watts, Cecil E. Professional Methods for Record Care and
    Use. New Hyde Park, New York: Elpa Marketing
    Industries Inc.

    This booklet is very good on proper record care
    and storage.

Whitaker, Rod. The Language of Film. Englewood Cliffs,
    New Jersey: Prentice-Hall, Inc., 1970.

    An excellent book to help you understand the power
    of visual and aural media combined.

White, James F. New Forms of Worship. Nashville, Tennessee:
    Abingdon Press, 1971.

    This is an excellent book dealing with the need for
    new forms in worship with many practical sugges-
    tions for accomplishing the goals of innovative
    worship. This book is a must for the minister
    interested in innovative worship.

White, James F. Protestant Worship and Church Architecture.
    New York: Oxford University Press, 1964.

    A very good book detailing how architecture forces
    much of our worship into a certain style and content.

Equipment

Cameras and Equipment

Canon
Bell & Howell Co.
7100 McCormick Road
Chicago, Illinois 60645

Eastman Kodak Co.
343 State Street
Rochester, New York 14650

Exakta Photo. Prod. Corp.
134 5th Avenue
New York, New York 10011

Honeywell Photographic (Pentax)
P. O. Box 22083
Denver, Colorado 80222

Konica Camera Corp.
Woodside, New York 11377

Leica/Leitz
E. Leitz, Inc.
Rockleigh, New Jersey 07647

Mamiya Div.
Ehrenreich Photo Opt. Ind., Inc.
Garden City, New York 11530

Minolta Corp.
200 Park Avenue So.
New York, New York 10003

Miranda
Allied Impex Corp.
Division of AIC Photo Inc.
Carle Place, New York 11514

Nikon, Inc.
Garden City, New York 11530

Olympus
Ponder & Best Inc.
11201 West Pico Blvd.
Los Angeles, Calif. 90064

Ricoh
Braun North America Dept. M-4
55 Cambridge Parkway
Cambridge, Mass. 02142

Rollier of America Inc.
100 Lehigh Drive
Fairfield, New Jersey 07006

Soligor Lenses
Allied Impex Corp.
168 Glen Cove Road
Carle Place, New York 11514

Vivitar Lenses
Ponder & Best, Inc.
11201 West Pico Blvd.
Los Angeles, Calif. 90064

Yashica Inc.
50-17 Queens Blvd.
Woodside, New York 11377

Projectors

2" x 2" Slide Projectors

Eastman Kodak Company
343 State Street
Rochester, New York 14650

GAF Corporation
AV Products Division
140 W. 51st Street
New York, New York 10020

Honeywell, Inc.
Photographic Products Division
A-V Department
5501 S. Broadway
Littleton,Colorado 80120

Overhead Projectors

American Optical Corp.
Eggert Road
Buffalo, New York 14215

Bell & Howell Co.
Audio Visual Division
7100 McCormick Road
Chicago, Illinios 60645

Beseler, Charles Company
219 South 18th Street
East Orange, New Jersey 07018

Buhl Projector Co., Inc.
Div. of Int. Ed. & Trng., Inc.
1776 New Hwy.
Farmingdale, New York 11725

GAF Corp.
A-V Prod. Div.
140 West 51st Street
New York, New York 10020

3M Company
Visual Prod. Div.
3M Center
St. Paul, Minn. 55101

Projection Optics Co.
271 11th Avenue
East Orange, New Jersey 07018

16 mm Projectors

Audio Visual Educational Systems, Inc.
5821 Ledbetter
Houston, Texas 77017

Bell & Howell Co.
Audio Visual Division
7100 McCormick Road
Chicago, Illinois 60645

Eastman Kodak Company
343 State Street
Rochester, New York 14650

Graflex Division
The Singer Company
3750 Monroe Avenue
Rochester, New York 14603

Honeywell, Inc.
Photographic Prod. Div A-V Dept.
5501 S. Broadway
Littleton, Colorado 80120

Kalart Victor Corporation
P. O. Box 112, Hultenius St.
Plainville, Conn. 06062

Viewlex Inc.
1 Broadway Avenue
Holbrook, L.I., New York 11741

Super 8 Projectors

Eastman Kodak Company
343 State Street
Rochester, New York 14650

GAF Corporation, A-V Prod. Div.
140 West 51st Street
New York, New York 10020

Honeywell, Inc.
Photo. Prod. Div., A-V Dept.
5501 S. Broadway
Littleton, Colorado 80120

Filmstrip Projectors

Audio Visual Educational Systems, Inc.
5821 Ledbetter
Houston, Texas 77017

Bell & Howell Co., A-V Division
7100 McCormick Road
Chicago, Illinois 60645

Graflex Division
The Singer Company
3750 Monroe Avenue
Rochester, New York 14603

Viewlex Inc.
1 Broadway Avenue
Holbrook, L.I., New York 11741

Screens

> Da-Lite Screen Co., Inc.
> P. O.Box 629
> Warsaw, Indiana 46580
>
> Draper Shade & Screen Co.
> 411 S. Pearl St.
> Spiceland, Indiana 47385
>
> Graflex Division
> The Singer Company
> 3750 Monroe Avenue
> Rochester, New York 14603
>
> International Audio Visual Inc.
> 119 Blanchard St.
> Seattle, Washington 98121
>
> Knox Manufacturing Co.
> 111 Spruce Street
> Wood Dale, Illinois 60191
>
> Pola Coat Inc.
> 9750 Conklin Road
> Cincinnati, Ohio 45242

Tape Recorders

> Ampex Corporation
> Magnetic Tape Division
> 401 Broadway
> Redwood City, Calif. 94063
>
> Song/Superscope
> 8150 Vineland Avenue
> Sun Valley, California 91352
>
> Wollensak/3M Co. Building
> 224-6 E, 3M Center
> St. Paul, Minn. 55101

Programmers and Dissolve Units

> Arion Corp.
> 825 Boone Avenue North
> Minneapolis, Minn. 55427

Eastman Kodak Co.
343 State St.
Rochester, New York 14650

Intermedia Systems Corp.
711 Mass. Avenue
Cambridge, Mass. 02139

Photosound Systems, Inc.
4444 W.76th St.
Minneapolis, Minn. 55435

MULTI-MEDIA SOURCES

American Library Color Slide Co., Inc.
305 East 45th Street
New York, New York 10017

> The most complete compilation of slides on all
> facets of art and archaeology.

Argus Communications
3505 North Ashland Avenue
Chicago, Illinois 60657

> Some very creative resources in many different
> media forms.

Kairos
Box 24056
Minneapolis, Minnesota 55424

> Some very creative multi-media resources are
> being produced by this company.

Society for Visual Education
1345 Diversey Parkway
Chicago, Illinois 60614

> A wide range of 2" x 2" slides, filmstrips, and
> other media resources. A selected group of art
> masterpieces on the life of Christ.

Space Photos
2608 Sunset
Houston, Texas 77005

> A wide range of pictures and slides on all

MULTI-MEDIA IN THE CHURCH

phases of space exploration.

Teleketics
Franciscan Communications Center
1229 South Santee Street
Los Angeles, California 90015

Some extremely good resources for celebration
worship are available here.

Thomas S. Klise Company
Box 3418
Peoria, Illinois 61614

A group of creative filmstrips which may be
used in many ways in multi-media worship.